Norms of Violence

Norms of Violence: Violent Socialization Processes and the Spillover Effect for Youth Crime explores the degree to which violent socialization processes, both at the macro- and micro-levels, are associated with youth criminal behavior. Based on a quantitative test of an integrated theory of social control and culture of violence, the author argues that violent socialization is a process involving physical violence, exposure to violence, and pro-violent communications. All three dimensions, in combination with national-level indicators of violence, contribute to a norm of violence which, at a national level, spills over into other dimensions of society, including the family environment.

This book seeks to answer if violent socialization processes truly control youth behavior. Various quantitative methods are used to demonstrate how violent socialization tends to be more prevalent in nations with indicators of violence compared to nations without such indicators. The spilling over of violence into socialization processes creates a context of violence normalized as a form of social control, which exacerbates youth criminal behavior within pro-violent nations.

This book is unique in propelling a more thorough explanation of international youth crime by focusing on both victimization (violent socialization) and offending, rather than arguing solely that victimization is a correlate of youth crime. It provides a reference point for future comparative research offering theoretical explanations for youth crime across different nations and is essential reading for those engaged in youth and juvenile justice efforts and scholars interested in issues surrounding violence, youth, and justice.

Aimée X. Delaney is Associate Professor of Criminal Justice at Worcester State University. Prior to working in academia, she was employed for many years in the American criminal/juvenile justice systems, including work in child protection, a special investigator in the State of New Hampshire, and manager of a juvenile diversion program specializing in alterative conflict resolution. She earned her PhD from the University of New Hampshire, under the direction and guidance of Dr. Murray Straus, Dr. Cesar Rebellon, and Dr. Melissa Wells.

Dr. Delaney has published in *Criminal Justice Review*, *Contemporary Perspectives in Family Violence*, *International Criminal Justice Review*, *International Journal of Offender Therapy and Comparative Criminology*, and *Sexual Harassment and Misconduct: An Encyclopedia* among other published works. Dr. Delaney is also the primary evaluator for a Drug-Free Community Grant, for which she has developed five different Youth Risk Behavior Surveys and analyzed data obtained from these surveys. She has written several policy publications and monographs related to work on this Drug-Free Community Grant.

Dr. Delaney's research focuses on family and community violence, focusing on risk factors associated with youth victimization and offending both within the United States and globally, and the impact of youth violence and victimization on the justice systems and communities. As an active member of the Academy of Criminal Justice Sciences and the Northeast Association of Criminal Justice Sciences, Dr. Delaney regularly presents her research at the annual meetings.

Routledge Studies in Juvenile Justice and Delinquency

Juvenile justice matters are of critical concern in both the United States and around the world. Books in the *Routledge Studies in Juvenile Justice and Delinquency* series explore mechanisms, consequences, insights, and innovations in the field of juvenile justice and its responses to delinquency. Each monograph will examine new areas of empirical and theoretical inquiry, provide an agenda-setting discussion of important concepts and controversies surrounding juvenile justice and delinquency, and seek to encompass a transnational or global approach to the issues addressed. The series will be a resource for the international community of undergraduates, postgraduates, researchers, practitioners, and policymakers concerned with juveniles and families caught up in or at risk of engagement in delinquency and justice system involvement.

Series editor David L. Myers

Contextual Characteristics in Juvenile Sentencing
Examining the Impact of Concentrated Disadvantage on Youth Court Outcomes
Rimonda Maroun

Due Process Protections for Youth
Defense Counsel Policies and Disparity in the Juvenile Justice System
Emily K. Pelletier

Norms of Violence
Violent Socialization Processes and the Spillover Effect for Youth Crime
Aimée X. Delaney

Routledge Studies in Juvenile Justice and Delinquency

Juvenile justice matters are of critical concern in both the United States and around the world. Books in the *Routledge Studies in Juvenile Justice and Delinquency* series explore mechanisms, consequences, insights, and innovations in the field of juvenile justice and its responses to delinquency. Each monograph will examine new areas of empirical and theoretical inquiry, provide an agenda-setting discussion of important concepts and controversies surrounding juvenile justice and delinquency, and seek to encompass a transnational or global approach to the issues addressed. The series will be a resource for the international community of undergraduates, postgraduates, researchers, practitioners, and policymakers concerned with juveniles and families caught up in or at risk of engagement in delinquency and justice system involvement.

Series editor David L. Myers

Contextual Characteristics in Juvenile Sentencing
Examining the Impact of Concentrated Disadvantage on Youth Court Outcomes
Rimonda Maroun

Due Process Protections for Youth
Defense Counsel Policies and Disparity in the Juvenile Justice System
Emily K. Pelletier

Norms of Violence
Violent Socialization Processes and the Spillover Effect for Youth Crime
Aimée X. Delaney

Norms of Violence

Violent Socialization Processes and the Spillover Effect for Youth Crime

Aimée X. Delaney

Routledge
Taylor & Francis Group
NEW YORK AND LONDON

First published 2021
by Routledge
605 Third Avenue, New York, NY 10017

and by Routledge
2 Park Square, Milton Park, Abingdon, Oxon, OX14 4RN

Routledge is an imprint of the Taylor & Francis Group, an informa business

Library of Congress Cataloging-in-Publication Data
Names: Delaney, Aimée X., author.
Title: Norms of violence : violent socialization processes and the spillover effect for youth crime / Aimée X. Delaney.
Description: 1 Edition. | New York : Routledge, 2021. |
Series: Routledge studies in juvenile justice and delinquency |
Includes bibliographical references and index.
Identifiers: LCCN 2020044901 (print) | LCCN 2020044902 (ebook) |
ISBN 9780367254889 (hardback) | ISBN 9780429288029 (ebook)
Subjects: LCSH: Socialization. | Violence. | Youth and violence. |
Criminal behavior.
Classification: LCC HM686 .D45 2021 (print) | LCC HM686 (ebook) |
DDC 303.6--dc23
LC record available at https://lccn.loc.gov/2020044901
LC ebook record available at https://lccn.loc.gov/2020044902

ISBN: 978-0-367-25488-9 (hbk)
ISBN: 978-0-367-71231-0 (pbk)

Typeset in Bembo
by Deanta Global Publishing Services, Chennai, India

I dedicate this book to Dr. Murray A. Straus. You were not just my professor, but a mentor and a friend. Your unwavering support and belief sustained me through a difficult yet challenging part of my life. I would never have been able to finish this without you.

Contents

Illustrations

Figures

Tables

Preface

This book explores the degree to which violent socialization processes, both at the macro-level and micro-level, are associated with youth criminal behavior. The premise of the book is a quantitative test of an integrated theory of social control and culture of violence. The focus of this book is to demonstrate empirical support for a new, integrated theory of social control-culture of violence, herein referred to as norms of violence. The main argument is that violent socialization, as a process involving physical violence, exposure to violence, and pro-violent communications, contributes to a norm of violence occurring within a context that fails to adequately control youth behavior. This context is national level acceptance of violence (macro-level) and spillover of this acceptance of violence into the family (micro-level), which inherently influences ineffective control over youths' behavior. The norms of violence theory is a tested cross-national analysis using a variety of quantitative methodologies. Data is from the International Dating Violence Study (Straus & Members of the International Dating Violence Research Consortium, 2004).

The book opens with a discussion on control of youth behavior through socialization processes, and how ineffective socialization processes contribute to youth crime. The theoretical premise is that socialization occurs within a context: when socialization involves violence, the context from the national level effect creates normative violence within a nation which then spills over into the family. In the second chapter, "Socialization processes as violent social control" offer a theoretical discussion on youth crime. Theories include learning, social control, and culture of violence. The discussion differentiates the theoretical explanations of violence and youth crime. The third chapter delves into the main argument of the book: the theoretical proposition that violence is normal within some nations creating a context for the acceptance of violence. This normalization of violence spills over into the socialization processes of families, which inherently contributes to the ineffective control of youth behavior. These "norms of violence" within familial socialization processes include violent discipline, exposure to violence, and violence-based communication. The fourth chapter introduces the dataset, sample, and variables/ measures operationalized as norms of violence as well as controls. Tests of reliability and validity are discussed. The specific analyses used to test norms of violence are also discussed: T-tests, correlations, regression analyses, factor analyses, and other statistical techniques explore variables of violent socialization and their association with youth crime both cross-nationally and internationally. The fifth chapter provides the analyses. The variation in youth criminal behavior from nation to nation can be viewed as part of a context of norms of violence, via spillover into the family. Youth from families that use violent socialization processes tend to engage in significantly more criminal behavior, compared to youth from families that use non-violent familial socialization processes. These results also occur at the national level: overall violent socialization is associated with increased mean youth criminal behavior scores across nations. In the last chapter of the book, the implications of norms of violence on social control are discussed. There are consequences for norms of violence within nations. These consequences include reduced social control and increased criminal behavior among youth. The discussion also includes a discussion of resources and policy changes that can be implemented to combat norms of violence across different nations.

This book provides a more thorough explanation of international youth crime. Most of the currently published books focus almost exclusively on explaining youth crime within the United States. While there are publications that offer some examination into correlates of youth crime across different nations, there appear to be no published books that seek to explain and test the context of normative socialized violence within nations that spill over into families and are associated with youth crime across different nations. Ultimately, violent socialization processes are a form of victimization, particularly as defined in this book. This book takes a unique approach by focusing on both victimization (violent socialization) and offending, rather than arguing solely that victimization is a correlate of youth crime. The subject matter of this book will appeal to multiple disciplines, including criminal justice, social work, sociology, anthropology, law and policy, family studies, and other social sciences. The book is written for scholars of criminological theory, researchers of family violence and other forms of violence, academics interested in research supporting new theories of juvenile crime, and graduate students. Further, this book provides a reference point for future comparative research examining youth crime across different nations and offering theoretical explanations for youth crime.

Acknowledgments

I would like to thank all the professors who have assisted me with learning about different aspects of this project and supported my efforts to complete this project throughout the years: Dr. David Finkelhor (University of New Hampshire and Crimes against Children Research Center), Dr. Rebecca Glauber (University of New Hampshire), Dr. Suzanne Graham (University of New Hampshire), Dr. Lawrence Hamilton (University of New Hampshire), Dr. Glenda Kaufman-Kantor (Family Research Lab/ Crimes against Children Research Center), Dr. Maureen McLeod (Sage Colleges), Mr. John Mockry (Clinton Community College), Dr. David Orrick (Norwich University), Dr. William Rogers (Hesser College), Dr. Cassandra Reyes (West Chester University), Dr. Lawrence Rosenberg (Millersville University), Dr. Tom Safford (University of New Hampshire), and Dr. Wendy Walsh (Crimes against Children Research Center). Certainly, this includes one of the most important group of people: my dissertation committee. Thank you, Dr. Michele Dillon (University of New Hampshire), Dr. Cesar Rebellon (University of New Hampshire), Dr. Erin Sharp (University of New Hampshire), Dr. Murray Straus (University of New Hampshire and Family Research Lab), and Dr. Melissa Wells (University of New Hampshire).

I have been fortunate enough to have received support from several professional organizations in order to work on and successfully complete portions of this project in the earliest stages. My gratitude is extended to the Academy of Criminal Justice Sciences, the Carsey Institute at the University of New Hampshire, the Northeast Association of Criminal Justice Sciences, and the Society for the Study of Social Problems. I have also been fortunate to receive the support of my editors, Dr Dave Myers (University of New Haven) and Ms Ellen Boyne (Routledge Publishing). Thank you for this opportunity.

Finally, no work is ever complete without the love of family and friends. Throughout the entire decade of this process, you have been my support. Thank you, Kathy. And to Tanner, I appreciate all your understanding and sacrifices to give me the time and space I needed to work on this book. You will always be my grace.

Chapter 1

Introduction

Violence is a powerful force within society. Violence is so influential that humans have been using violence to resolve all methods of conflict for centuries, perhaps millennia. Violence is not viewed as a problem within some nations, but may in fact be considered normal (Eller, 2006). Each nation embraces very different norms surrounding the acceptability of violence. Violence tends to occur within a context influenced by social norms (O'Keefe, 2007; Palmeri, Sams, & Turcotte, 2004; Rosario, Salzinger, Feldman, & Ng-Mak, 2003). For example, male youth violence has been associated with violence occurring within the context of violent neighborhoods and norms for neighborhood violence (Reed, 2008). The inference is that youth violence occurs within a context.

Traditionally, criminologists have examined violence and crime through an individualistic perspective—it has been seen as an antisocial behaviorial issue among certain people within society—rather than examine the contextual factors and effects that surround these individual people (Crump, 2017) and the groups to which they belong. Youth are exposed to many groups within society, and the norms emitted through those groups. This includes national-level norms, influences from a nation that create a context of norms in which youth are socialized. These norms are established by the methods in which social institutions act and react towards members of society. This may include law and government, as well as the family and other major social institutions in which socialization processes normalize certain behaviors.

Some national-level norms are consistent, regardless of regional variation, and set the tone for norms within society. Violence tends to occur within a context influenced by social norms (O'Keefe, 2007; Palmeri, Sams, & Turcotte, 2004; Rosario, Salzinger, Feldman, & Ng-Mak, 2003), and thus may be one of these consistent national-level norms. Norms accepting violence, then, occur as a contextual effect within any given nation. This contextual effect creates a national based normative standard: the degree to which violence is an acceptable norm within that nation. Such national-based normative standards become part of the primary factors that shape socialization of youth.

The family is still held primarily responsible for instilling control within and over youth as a mechanism to ensure conformity to the "moral standards and society's laws" (Schmalleger & Bartollas, 2008, p. 248). The family takes cues from norms set forth within a nation. These cues influence the methods in which families socialize their children. Parents who are unable to recognize violence as a manifestation of deviance may endorse the acceptance of violence within their socialization of youth. Perhaps violence is not inherently deviant within a nation. Instead, violence may be a normative standard within a nation. Such macro-level norms may spill over to families and further reinforce a context that shapes youth actions and reactions towards other members of society. These processes become violent socialization.

Violent socialization processes are multiple dimensions of violence that occur as part of the normative socialization of youth. These processes include violent discipline (i.e., the use of excessive physical discipline), exposure to violence, and pro-violent communication (e.g., advising youth to use violence to resolve conflict). These processes, in combination with other national based indicators of violence, form a context in which violence is a normative standard within society and infiltrates the socialization of youth. This book sets forth the justification for the theoretical proposition of norms of violence to explain variation in juvenile crime across different nations. The context of normative violence within a nation, particularly socialization processes involving the normalization of violence, contributes to youth criminal behavior.

The Context of Socialization

Socialization is a collective process which imparts the normative manner of behavior to members of society. It involves shared ways of thinking and behaving. Socialization is necessary to inculcate culture and transmit this culture on to future generations. The social structure of a nation is comprised of different social groups, clusters of social institutions. These institutions extend from the family level to the national level (e.g., government). Each institution holds roles and responsibilities in the socialization of youth. All aspects of a nation's social structure contribute to and are involved in socialization processes. Thus, individual members of society are not socialized independently. Socialization occurs within a context.

The context of socialization involves processes within families, communities, and the nation. Familial socialization process may be overt and direct (e.g., discipline to correct unwanted behavior). Communal socialization process may take on a subtler approach, through overt yet indirect methods. An example might be community members advising youth to use violence to resolve conflict (e.g., "hit them back" type of response). Aggregation of common communal socialization process may reflect national norms. Nationwide socialization processes are demonstrated through formal means that are both indirect and covert. Nations construct shared meanings throughout the socialization process in order to ensure that members conform to norms. These national-level meanings can spillover into the community. For example, the death penalty is a formality in some nations. These nations sanction governmental use of homicide as one response to individuals who violate laws. This knowledge is transmitted to members of that nation. Whether implicit or explicit, this type of violent conflict resolution is indoctrinated as a customary manner for conflict resolution. This "correction and guidance" (Eller, 2006, p. 54) over time can establish a pro-violent culture. Since inculcation into a nation's culture is necessary to ensure the functioning membership of society, violence can become an accepted standard within society.

Violence

Violence is a social fact. Any aspect of society that is functional, i.e., having a purpose of serving society, is a social fact (*cf.* Durkheim, 1977 [1914]). Some have argued that violence serves a useful purpose (Iadicola, 2012). Violence has been used to achieve goals, as the driving factor of accomplishment (Aronson, 2012). Violence may also be a method of conflict resolution (Linsky, Bachman, & Straus, 2004). Under such conditions, violence may even be structural. Structural violence refers to violence built into the organization of society (Iadicola, 2012) and the "means of the institutions, practices, instructions of society" that promote violence (Eller, 2006, p. 140). Violence occurs within every nation (Felitti et al., 1998; Reza, Mercy, & Krug, 2001; World Health Organization, 2002). Many nations engage in some type of structural violence, whether it is formal laws or informal practices. This makes violence, to some degree, a norm.

Expanding on the issue of violence as a social fact, defining violence can be challenging. Consideration must be made for the inherent issues with defining violence (Eller, 2006; Iadicola, 2012; Thornton, Voigt, & Harper, 2013). Several aspects of violence need to be considered in the conceptualization of violence: force, intention, legitimacy, and perspective.

Force can be defined as constraints exerted on others (Merriam-Webster, 2020). With this definition, everyone engages in force to some extent. Nations exert force on their members through the government. For example, some governments engage the use of capital punishment on members who violate laws. The government can use force to end human life, yet has laws against members of that nation committing homicide. What level of nation-sanctioned force is acceptable, but not acceptable, when enacted by other groups? This can be interpreted as biased structural violence: certain social institutions and their members may use violence, via force, against the members of that nation as a justification for maintaining the social order. Eller (2006) discusses structural violence as depriving people of choice while at the same time subjecting people to unfavorable conditions. Is this not the condition of all youth? Historically, minor youth were considered property and parents/other adult community figures had unrestricted authority to do to a child whatever was deemed necessary to control their behavior (Greven, 1992; Heywood, 2010). Minor youth had no recourse, regardless of the severity of the parents' actions (Champion, Merlo, & Benekos, 2015). In modern times, do youth have the choice to *not* be "spanked" or physically disciplined in every nation? If not, youth are exposed to conditions in which they are deprived of choice and condemned to physical assault. Youth are victims of structural violence. When force is mutual, such as using violence against someone who acted violently first, how do we differentiate between a perpetrator and a victim? Aren't adults who advise youth to use violence to resolve violence endorsing force?

There is also the consideration of intention. Eller (2006) and Iadicola (2012) argue that intention is not always necessary to define violence. Violence can be unintentional. For example, child abuse can be unintentionally manifested within the socialization practices, such as the use of physical discipline to correct youth's unwanted behaviors (e.g., see Bauman & Friedman, 1998; Eriksson, 2010; Forjuoh & Zwi, 1998; Hamby, Finkelhor, Turner, & Ormrod, 2011; Lee, & Kim, 2011; Pinheiro, 2006; Sousa, et al., 2011 for a more robust discussion of physical discipline as child abuse). The argument can be made that this is a necessary correction to control youth behavior. The intent of this method of socialization is to raise youth to be productive members of society. Violence may not be the intent. But hitting is nonetheless violence. Therefore, intent need not be instrumental in the conceptualization of violence.

Eller (2006) argues that legitimacy concerns the "relativity" of violence. Specifically, is violence relevant? Some nations may be more tolerant of violence and this tolerance is reflected within the social structure. This may include laws and socialization processes. Violence may also be expressed through behaviors, such as the rate of violent crime. The relativity of violence depends on the degree to which the members of a nation collectively accept violence. Members of a nation may justify violence (Iadicola, 2012). What is viewed as wrong for one nation may be a norm within another nation (Eller, 2006). While not all nations legitimize violence, violence may be a norm without the social groups being consciously aware.

This leads to the last aspect of defining violence: perspective. Perspective involves the collective viewpoint of members of a nation. These perspectives can be reflected in the customs of society, both formal and informal. Laws serve as formal customs, reflecting norms through what members of a nation deem to be deviant and the sanctions associated with such deviance. Methods used to socialize youth are informal customs. The specific techniques used to inculcate youth into the nation's culture can also reflect that nation's overall perspective if these methods are engaged collectively across that society. For example, if it is common among families and communities to advise youth to use violence to resolve conflict, youth become inculcated into a culture that promotes violence. Pro-violent messages are the collective viewpoint, and may become part of the techniques used to socialize youth. Pro-violence is not a socially desirable perspective for social groups in a nation. But even if the different social groups are not consciously aware of the perspective, or outright deny the perspective, the collective viewpoint still exists.

Taking into consideration these issues, violence is defined as behavior expended to inflict harm on another. This definition is consistent with others' definitions of violence (e.g., see Iadicola, 2012; Thornton, Voigt, & Harper, 2013). Violent behavior includes direct action towards another, exposing another to violent behavior, and words encouraging others to engage in direct action against another. All of these actions can inflict harm, either directly or vicariously. Harm can be physical, psychological, and social. Physical harm holds as much negative consequences as psychological and social pain (Chen, Williams, Fitness, & Newton, 2008; Conejero, Olié, Calati, Ducasse, & Courtet, 2018; Nesse & Schulkin, 2019; Xu, Zuo, Wang, & Han, 2009; Zhang, Barreto, & Doyle, 2019; Zhang, Zhang, & Kong, 2019). This is because the harm stems from the use of force, particularly when the violence is deemed as legitimate and is part of the perspective of the nation. Force is simply exerting one's will onto another. This force may not be intentional, as discussed previously. But engaging in violent behaviors towards or around another is still exerting one's will. Behavior need not necessarily be intentional towards a specific recipient to be considered violence. Again, intention is not necessary to inflict harm. For example, violence exposure is not always outright intended, yet can still inflict harm on another. Youth who witness violence between adults may still be harmed even when those adults did not intend the youth to see their violence, nor were they motivated to inflict harm on the youth. This is not to imply that the violence discussed here is accidental. The violence is purposeful to some extent, such as when adults intend to harm each other through violence. The purpose of the violence may have been directed towards another, but such violence is displaced when others are exposed to the violence. This exposure can cause harm.

Some may argue that there has been a reduction in violence over the years. Violence is difficult to measure, particularly over time (Eller, 2006; Ember & Ember, 1994; Iadicola, 2012; Thornton, Voigt, & Harper, 2013). Social perspectives of violence mostly remain an image of physical action by one person to another person. This may be the reason members of society have the misperception of a decrease in violence. But definitions of what constitutes violence have evolved. Other definitions of violence encompass physical force (Thornton, Voigt, & Harper, 2013) to harm caused within the social order (Iadicola, 2012). Some may also argue that violence is culturally relative (*cf.* Eller, 2006). But violence needs to be defined universally (Iadicola, 2012), and there are universal indicators of violence transnationally. Behaviors considered violent, to some extent in certain spheres of life, are common across all nations. As an example, the forced killing of a human being is generally considered violent. This is the premise of capital punishment: the government kills a member of society by force. Members of society legitimize this behavior. If a forced killing is committed by a group of people behaving as vigilantes, these same members of society may argue such behavior is illegitimate. Both situations involve intended violence. Justifications for forced killings are irrelevant in terms of defining an act of violence. In fact, it gives strength to the argument that violence is normalized in some nations.

There are many factors that may contribute to the normalization of violence within a nation. It would be easy to argue that "terrorism" is a form of violence. But how do we define terrorism? There is no universal definition of terrorism (White, 2017). It is just as easy to argue "war" is an act of violence. What is the difference between war and terrorism? Terrorism and war may involve some acts of violence, but many definitions for terrorism and war hold singular perspectives. These definitions are based on the perspective of the victor, and the victor often legitimizes their acts of violence while vilifying the actions of the defeated. Terrorism and war have factors varying from nation to nation, and do not occur universally across nations. Therefore, these concepts cannot be reliably measured as an indicator of violence transnationally. There are many other concepts that can be argued. However, most concepts are not universally experienced transnationally. Violent socialization processes are both universal and experienced across many nations. Violent socialization processes meet all three of these characteristics of violence.

Violent Socialization Processes

Violent socialization processes include multiple different violence-based actions implemented to inculcate youth into the norms of society. These processes include three dimensions: physical discipline, exposure to violence, and pro-violence communication. These processes are conceptualized as the combination of interdependent methods infused with violence used to control youth behavior.

Violent Discipline

Violent discipline involves physical discipline that is frequent and occurs during both childhood and adolescence. Some have suggested that the purpose of physical discipline is to prevent youth from overreaching the boundaries of acceptable behavior, to correct unacceptable behavior, or change undesirable behavior (Gagné, et al., 2007; Socolar & Stein, 1995). Such arguments are outdated. The current body of research, across multiple disciplines and spanning decades, indicates that hitting other people, regardless of status or context, is violence (e.g., Bauman & Friedman, 1998; Crosson-Tower, 2008; Eriksson, 2010; Forjuoh & Zwi, 1998; Hamby, Finkelhor, Turner, & Ormrod, 2011; Lee & Kim, 2011; Pinheiro, 2006; Sousa, et al., 2011; Straus & Donnelly, 1994; Taylor, Hamvas, & Paris, 2011; Zolotor, et al., 2008). In fact, the United Nations (2006a) includes physical discipline in the definition of violence against children. There is a fine line between what constitutes discipline and the physical abuse of youth. Many experts define extreme discipline as the excessive and frequent physical discipline of children (e.g., see Greven, 1992; Payne, Higgins, & Blackwell, 2010; Taylor, Hamvas, & Paris, 2011; Zolotor et al., 2008), and have come to see physical discipline as ineffective (e.g., Capaldi, Chamberlain, & Patterson, 1997; Gershoff, & Bitensky, 2007). Thus, excessive physical discipline, if used on youth consistently, may actually be violence rather than a means of discipline to control youth behavior. This makes physical discipline an important dimension within a typology of violent socialization processes.

Exposure to Violence

Another dimension of violent socialization processes involves consistent exposure to violence. Witnessing violence may suggest to youth normative standards of violence within families and communities. Regular and consistent environments of violence create a context in which violence becomes normalized. The violence need not be directed at the youth, nor be directly related to the discipline of youth, yet violence is still part of youth's socialization in the sense of promoting pro-violent identification. The family, as a primary socializing agent (Kendall, 2010), is responsible for instilling limitations of unacceptable behavior and the community is expected to reinforce such limitations on youth behavior. Youth should identify violence against others as wrong, based in the laws of a nation, because effective socialization instills a sense of self-control (*cf.* Gottfredson & Hirschi, 1990).

Pro-violent Messages

Communication endorsing violence is the third dimension of violent socialization processes. Pro-violent messages involve adults telling youth to respond to violence with their own violence. For example, a youth may be told to hit someone who hits or insults them. In general, such advice tends to be a deviant belief within contemporary mainstream societies (Ohene, Ireland, McNeely, & Borowsky, 2006). As argued by Gottfredson and Hirschi (1990), parents who do not recognize deviant behavior do not engage in effective socialization. This argument can be extended to community members who engage in socialization processes of youth, such as teachers or peers' parents. Communications need to demonstrate the recognition of norms of society rather than support deviance (Gorman-Smith & Tolan, 1998). Consistent pro-violent messages may instill a sense that violence is an acceptable means to resolve conflict (Straus & Donnelly, 1994). These adults are not encouraging the development of self-control, nor are they exerting control over youth behavior. Youth may instead internalize an identification with violence normalcy from receiving such pro-violent messages.

These three dimensions, violent discipline, exposure to violence, and pro-violent messages, constitute a typology of violent socialization. These processes cannot be separated out into singular dimensions. Examining the effects of a singular dimension of violent socialization, such as physical discipline, cannot fully explain criminal behavior. Again, violent socialization processes are interdependent, violent methods of control that hinder the ability to prevent youth criminal behavior. Experienced together, this typology of violent socialization is expected to increase criminal behavior among youth, as youth may internalize the underlying significance of violence as a normative standard.

Violent Socialization and Crime

The perpetration of violence is not conducive to socialization that effectively inculcates control among youth. The presence of violent methods of control has been shown to actively contribute to youth's criminal behavior. Youth chronically exposed to violence are more likely to engage in violent behavior later in life than those youth who were not exposed to violence (Forbes & Adams-Curtis, 2001; Margolin & Gordis, 2000; Spano, Rivera, & Bolland, 2010). Yet, most of the currently published research explores the relationship between singular aspects of violence and criminal behavior (e.g., see Brezina, 1998; Robertson, Baird-Thomas, & Stein, 2008). Explanations for youth crime require the study of interdependent relationships among multiple social factors (Baker, 2010).

The current literature suggests a general relationship between violent discipline and criminal behavior (e.g., Goddard, Goff, Melancon, & Huebner, 2000; Teague, Mazerolle, Legosz, & Sanderson, 2008), including youth criminal behavior (e.g., Rebellon & Van Gundy, 2005; Robertson, Baird-Thomas, & Stein, 2008). In a review of published research spanning 100 years, Gershoff (2008) shows that youth who experienced physical discipline frequently or severely are more likely to use physical violence as adults in various intimate relationships. This literature review was focused solely on the use of physical discipline towards youth and did not include other aspects of violent socialization processes. The issue with these studies is the measures do not fully represent violent socialization processes, focusing instead on a singular aspect. However, the research demonstrates, consistently, that physical discipline is a violent method of control (Straus & Donnelly, 1994). Physical discipline, ultimately, offers little to no control over youth's behavior as it fails to properly socialize youth.

Violent Familial Socialization Processes and Criminal Behavior

There is a direct link between exposure to family violence and delinquency (Hamby, Finkelhor, Turner, & Ormrod, 2011; Herrenkohl, et al., 2003; Smith & Thornberry, 1995). Violence within the family often manifests concurrently and in multiple different ways (Crosson-Tower, 2008). Family violence can manifest as physical discipline, exposure to violence, and parents communicating pro-violence messages.

There is an abundance of research supporting the link between physical discipline and youth criminal behavior (Robertson, Baird-Thomas, & Stein, 2008). Even in the presence of social control (e.g., attachments, self-control), this result remains consistent (Rebellon & Van Gundy, 2005; Teague, Mazerolle, Legosz, & Sanderson, 2008). This indicates that physical discipline is ineffective at instilling control over youth behavior. Most studies focus on experiences with physical abuse by a parent, such as being beaten up, using a weapon, and injuries requiring hospitalization. While physical abuse can be extreme, not all physical punishment involves such an extremity. A more robust measure of experiences with physical discipline is the degree to which physical discipline occurs over time.

Further, not all studies measure actual crime and instead focuse on status offenses. For example, Robertson, Baird-Thomas, and Stein (2008) measured delinquency as (1) school suspensions, without clarifying the reason for the suspension, (2) gang membership,[1] and (3) prior detentions. None of these meausres indicate true criminal behavior. Such studies cannot draw correlations between physical abuse and youth criminal behavior with confidence if criminal behavior is not included as a measure. To avoid validity issues with definitions of crime, offenses need to be considered crime universally regardless of youths' status.

Youth who are exposed to violence within their family tend to act out violently towards others (e.g., Forbes & Adams-Curtis, 2001; Margolin & Gordis, 2000; Spano, Rivera, & Bolland, 2010) and engage in criminal behavior (Hamby, Finkelhor, Turner, & Ormrod, 2011; Herrenkohl, et al., 2003; Smith & Thornberry, 1995). Many studies examine exposure to family violence without also examining other manifestations of violence. A study that looked at the combined effects of physical abuse and exposure to family violence found that each singular aspect of family violence alone was not associated with youth criminal behavior but the combined effects of physical abuse *and* exposure to family violence were significantly associated with youth crime (Sousa, et al., 2011). It is worth noting that in this study, the sample is derived from a limited group of young children in the Lehigh Longitudinal Study (see Herrenkohl, Herrenkohl, Egolf, & Wu, 1991). Most of these children were from child welfare programs in two counties within Pennsylvania already at high risk for criminal behavior. Given the limited scope of this sample, a more general population is necessary.

Communication is important in understanding the control of deviant behavior (Ellickson & Morton, 1999), including criminal behavior. While there appear to be no published studies that examine the relationship between violent communication and criminal behavior specifically, there are some analogous studies related to parental recognition of deviant behavior and violent behavior among youth. In one study of Nigerian parents, more than one-quarter (26.2%) answered that they would advise their child to use violence to retaliate against another youth hitting or teasing them (Ojo, Akintomide, & Omoyemiju,

2011). In fact, although considered deviant, parents from this area of Nigeria are known, traditionally, to engage in pro-violent messages because this type of violent communication has occurred repeatedly over multiple generations (Ojo, Akintomide, & Omoyemiju, 2011). The results of Ojo, Akintomide, and Omoyemiju's study clearly do not match the "common knowledge" of this specific nation. This may be due to social desirability, which was not controlled for in the study. Parents may not want to admit openly that they tell youth to engage in violence as a means of resolving conflict at school. Perhaps a better approach to capturing such sensitive information is to inquire *of the youth* if they were told by their parents to engage in violence if another youth insults or hits them.

In another study, within the United States, more than one-third of parents (38.1%) with youth who had diagnosed mental health issues reported they would advise the use of violence if their child was hit by another youth (Ohene, Ireland, McNeely, & Borowsky, 2006). The chance of the youth within this study engaging in violent behavior towards other youth was probably present prior to the research, given that this study sampled only youth who had been identified as having psychosocial behavioral problems prior to administration of the survey. As such, the results could possibly be linked to factors other than parents' pro-violent messages. Nonetheless, these parents may have failed to exert control over and instill self-control in their youth by using pro-violent messages.

The review of the literature is clear: "less parental behavioral control equals more problem behavior" (Vazsonyi & Flannery, 1997, p. 98). Familial socialization is widely supported in predicting and controlling youth criminal behavior (Schmalleger & Bartollas, 2008). With the causes of criminal behavior being diverse and complex (Church, Wharton, & Taylor, 2009; Edwards, 1996), the currently published literature tends to neglect the combination of multiple dimensions of violent familial socialization that *together* fail to control youth behavior and positively influence youth crime. But risk for youth criminal behavior may not result exclusively from socialization within the family. More research is needed to understand the role of violent familial socialization on youth criminal behavior, particularly in consideration that socialization occurs within contexts.

National Contexts of Violent Socialization Processes and Criminal Behavior

The circumstance of life within any given nation is likely to vary. This variance may include a context in which violence may be more common within some nations. What if violent socialization processes are contextually based within specific nations? Would violent socialization processes at a community-based level be ineffective at controlling criminal behavior among youth in the same manner as violent familial socialization processes? As abundant as the research may be linking socialization and youth criminal behavior, there is a dearth of research examining the impact of socialization processes on youth behavior transnationally. There appears to be no published studies that have examined the contextual effect of both familial and community level violent socialization processes on youth crime transnationally. But more information is needed to understand the range of risk factors and pathways for criminal behavior (Shortt, Low, Capaldi, Eddy, & Tiberio, 2017).

Some analogous research has identified the unique context in which certain national norms shape socialization processes (e.g., Greenfield, Flores, Davis, & Salimkhan, 2008; Keller, Otto, Lamm, Yovsi, & Kartner, 2008; Runyan et. al., 2010). Lee and Kim (2011) found that some youth in Korea were unable to recall experiences with physical abuse. Instead, youth who reported experiences mirroring physical abuse viewed the behaviors they endured in multiple different settings (e.g., family, school) as "discipline" rather than "violence." Lee and Kim (2011) attributed this finding to the unique context of Korea, in that violence towards children, particularly under the guise of discipline, is more tolerated in Korea compared to other nations. According to a summary report by several experts within the United States, "cultural/ethnic practices and beliefs are known to have an immense effect on what is considered as the norm" (Analytical Sciences, 2002, p. 10). Might such a context of violence exist across other nations?

Contextual Effect of Living within a Specific Nation

It has been argued that humans are particularly aggressive (Aronson, 2012). And, there are few nations that can claim to be exclusively nonviolent (Eller, 2006). Thus, violence may be more prevalent within some nations. Within nations, there are systems of networks, via families, friends, neighbors, and other informal associations, that influence and shape socialization processes (Kasarda & Janowitz, 1974). In this sense, socialization may occur with the context of the norms of the nation. The norms of that nation may be favorable for violent control over youth behavior.

Cross-national research is one of the most important areas in which to continue research that examines aspects of community life that may have a bearing on the socialization processes of families (Rutter, 1981). Yet, little international research exists to support the premise of a national based context of violence spilling over into socialization processes. The social sciences cannot advance understanding of nation-based processes unless there is more international research. Specifically, research needs to examine social phenomenon through national context effects that identify similarities within the same nation, while also recognizing variation both within the same nation and across different nations (Sellers, Kübler, Walter-Rogg, & Walks, 2012).

Do violent socialization processes occurring within a context of norms of violence within a nation effectively prevent youth crime or contribute to youth crime? This book seeks to answer this question, by illuminating the contextual effect of norms of violence within and across different nations. This contextual effect refers to conditions of violence within nations that contribute to methods of social control used by families and communities. Answering these questions will begin to fill gaps in the current international literature on violence by exploring an understanding of the context in which violence is infused into socialization processes, both within families and the community. Further, the research offered in this book will support the need to extend the conceptual framework of culture of violence and social control theories to explain how norms of violence ineffectively control youth behavior and contribute to criminal behavior. Many criminological theories have attempted to explain youth crime. Yet most of these theories take a limited approach in time and space to explain youth criminal behavior.

Note

1 Gang membership in and of itself does not always connote involvement in criminal behavior.

Chapter 2

Theoretical Explanations of Socialization Processes and Youth Criminal Behavior

There are several different theories that attempt to explain juvenile crime. These theories include social control theories, culture-based theories, and learning theories.

Social Control Theories

Social control theories argue, in general, youth must be controlled to repress criminal tendencies. Otherwise, youth naturally gravitate toward criminal behavior. Control is formulated through two outlets: external control (e.g., relationships, commitments) and internal control (e.g., internalization of society's values, norms). These controls prevent youth from violating legal codes, by encouraging conformity among youth. The theories suggest that if youth are tied into the community and they internalize communal codes, youth will voluntarily limit criminal behavior.

The main source for external control and indoctrinating youth with internal control is the family. It is the extent to which the family controls youth behavior, and encourages self-regulation in the absence of that external control, which prevents criminal behavior (e.g., see Nye & Weeks, 1956; Reiss, 1951; Reckless, 1967; Hirschi, 1969; Gottfredson & Hirschi, 1990; Hirschi, 2004). The family needs to develop conditions in which youth are obligated to conform to normative expectations for social behavior, including adherence to the law (*cf.* Durkheim, 1977 [1914]). However, the family does not operate in isolation. There are other agents of socialization within the youth community (immediate and nationwide) that contribute to control over youth behavior and may encourage the development of internal controls. Without such conditions, youth succumb to their impulses, violating social norms and laws (Hirschi, 1969).

The main argument of social control theories of crime is that motivation is constant for all youth. Social control theories seek to understand how it is possible to reduce the likelihood of youth engaging in criminal behavior and does not consider motivational issues. In essence, these are theories explaining the prevention of crime. Social control theories make a fundamental distinction from other theories of crime: youth are naturally prone toward criminal behavior. This natural proclivity needs to be controlled by the family. Motivation is not relevant in the explanation of criminal behavior. These theories explain why some youth *do not* commit crime. The degree to which prevention is possible varies as youth differ in their level of control, both externally and internally. The different restraints youth face in society explain variation in juvenile crime. Some youth may be less constrained to engage in criminal behavior compared to others because the controls that are supposed to be in place to prevent crime are lacking or missing. These controls are explained within different contexts depending on the specific control theory. But one aspect of control that this group of theories has in common is socialization.

Social control explanations for criminal behavior use measures of socialization to explain why some youth do not engage in criminal behavior compared to the youth who do engage in criminal behavior. Control over youth behavior, both external and internal, is developed through various socialization processes (Boyd & Higgins, 2006; De Li, 2004; Morris, Gerber, & Menard, 2011; Schoepfer & Piquero, 2006). Social institutions serve to regulate individual behavior, constrain individual impulses, and neutralize tendencies toward criminal behavior by properly socializing children at young ages.[1] Social control theories contend that familial socialization processes pose the most influential control over youth behavior. When families fail to effectively socialize youth, youth may be unable to self-regulate their behavior (Nye & Weeks, 1956), lack restraint, and engage in criminal behavior. The limitations of poor socialization processes include criminal behavior. While this argument is relatively consistent across social control theories, each iteration of these theories takes a different approach to explaining the preventative nature of socialization.

Criminological research has consistently identified a number of variables associated with the interdependent relationship of familial socialization. Specifically, these variables include attachments (e.g., Barnes et al., 2006; Bjarnason, Thorlindsson, Sigfusdottir, & Welch, 2005; Bui, 2009; Goetting, 1994; Herrenkohl, Huang, Tajima, & Whitney, 2003; Luthar & Goldstein, 2008; Matherne & Thomas, 2001; Parker & Benson, 2004; Turner, Hartman, & Bishop, 2007) and self-control (e.g., Gibson, Morris, & Beaver, 2009; Grasmick, Tittle, Bursik, & Arneklev, 1993; Piquero & Bouffard, 2007; Rebellon, Straus & Medeiros, 2008). Social bonds theories focus on the role of attachments, and a general theory of crime addresses self-control.

Social Bonds Theory

Hirschi's social control theory of "social bonds" (*cf.*, Hirschi, 1969) argues that the tight bonds to communal social groups (e.g., family, school, peers) prevent youth from engaging in criminal behavior. Of these communal social groups, the family is stressed as the most important institution in which to properly socialize youth to prevent crime. One familial socialization process that should effectively develop attachments is parental affection. Parental affection can include help and nurturance toward youth. If the family, and particularly parents, displays affection and support toward youth, this should create a bond. Youth may want to maintain the affection and support of the family. Consequently, youth do not engage in behavior that might disappoint their family and weaken this bond. Cohesive familial relationships are integral for the effective functioning of the family (Erikson, 1950) and criminological research has consistently shown that increased family support, such as closeness, love, and attachment, is associated with less criminal behavior (e.g., Bao, Haas, & Pi, 2007; Bjarnason, Thorlindsson, Sigfusdottir, & Welch, 2005; Matherne & Thomas, 2001; Parker & Benson, 2004). Hence, attachments are an important aspect of familial socialization that serves to control youth behavior.

The processes of socialization create conditions that insulate youth from criminal behavior. The conditions include attachment, commitment, involvement, and beliefs. As discussed, attachments are the supportive relationships between members of society. Youth make connections with family, adults, peer, and other members of the community, and these connections serve as a protective factor for youth behavior. Hirschi's argument is that it is the degree to which youth are invested in the people surrounding them, in relationships with others, which prevents criminal behavior. Commitment entrails the degree to which youth are dedicated to engaging in the conventional pathways of society. This includes having a connection to mainstream societal conventions in which youth do not want to jeopardize their investment in their status within the community. Involvement encompasses how much youth are active within conventional society. Being active and busy in conventional activities restricts youths' opportunities to engage in criminal behavior. And belief is the extent to which youth hold respect for and conscribe to the norms of society, such as the law. The acceptance of the social norms regulating conduct is purported to prevent youth criminal behavior. According to Social Bonding Theory (Hirschi, 1969) individuals who are attached, committed, involved, and believe form social bonds with other members of society and this bond prevents criminal behavior.

When these characteristics of social bonds are lacking, criminal behavior will emerge. Although Hirschi does not expressly discuss the macro-level effect, it can be inferred that the formation of collective social bonds serves to prevent youth criminal behavior across society, by controlling youth's actions. This may be reasoned as youth without bonds may gravitate toward other "unbonded" youth in an effort to establish a bond, even if that bond is based on criminal behavior. But Hirschi's failure to address the context in which social bonds occur is problematic. The theory does not consider macro-level factors, such as sociopolitical contexts, in which socialization occurs within communities and nations.

Instead, the family is considered as the primary socialization agent. The family is the main social institution charged with providing proper socialization to children. Social bonds theory should provide valuable insights into intrafamilial relationships. Hirschi (1969) makes a generic argument, to the effect, that the more attached youth are to various social groups the more likely youth are to refrain from becoming involved in criminal behavior. However, youth can hold familial attachments even when the family engages in violent socialization. The family can be supportive of the youth, providing understanding to the youth and helping the youth with problems they experience, while failing to support the development of self-control because the methods of control engaged by the parents involve violence. Violent socialization could theoretically be argued as a form of child victimization (Hamby, Finkelhor, Turner, & Ormrod, 2011), as directing violence toward children and exposing children to violence are considered manifestations of child maltreatment. These families are, at the very least, dysfunctional (Negriff, 2020). Studies have found that violent discipline (e.g., hitting or slapping the youth) significantly contributes to criminal behavior even when there were parent-child attachments (Johnson et al., 2011). Despite the potential harm of violence in the family, youth still form attachments with their family. Engaging in violent familial socialization processes does not negate the formation of attachments, but these attachments may not necessarily be effective at controlling youth behavior.

Second, all other components of social bonds theory involve norms within society. Norms that support violence may be counterproductive to social bonds. Youth can subscribe to the conventional pathways of society and, at the same time, reinforce violent socialization processes by encouraging the use of violence to resolve conflict. Such violence can include criminal behavior. Youth can be active within conventional society. Active involvement with other people is conducive to experiencing conflict at some point within the social interactions with others. If the norms of society encourage violent methods to resolve conflict, youth may use violence in their social exchanges of conflict. Therefore, active involvement in conventional activities will not restrict youths' opportunities to engage in criminal behavior. And, continuous exposure to culturally endorsed violence may encourage the development of pro-violent belief systems. These belief systems may lead youth to re-create the normative standards of violence within a nation. For example, nation-based laws supporting violence are formal norms. This includes socialization (Cohn & White, 1990). Such formal norms feed into the collective thought processes of society. The symbolic exchange of formal norms within socialization processes may influence the belief systems of members of society, as members of society only recognize such membership by taking the perspective of other people (*cf.* Mead, 1934). A person's investment in societal conformity, then, may encourage the reproduction of violence. The conformity is to the collective norms and beliefs of society. Social bonds theory does not consider the long-term effects of socialization as an interactive role. Hence, social bonding theory fails to account for the effect of *all* socialization processes.

Attachments within the family are formed through the socialization process (e.g., Bowlby, 1969; Bowlby, 1973). Through socialization, parents exert informal social control and instill in their children an ability to avoid instantaneously gratifying behavior, including crime. And the opposite is true: poor parent–child interactions are associated with criminal behavior (e.g. Aichhorn, 1963; Goetting, 1994; Herrenkohl, Huang, Tajima & Whitney, 2003; Hurrelman, 1990; Johnson & Pandina, 1991; Pittman & Chase-Lansdale, 2001; Sokol-Katz, Dunham, & Zimmerman, 1997). But attachments *alone* are not necessarily associated with the prevention of criminal behavior (Brezina, 1998). Other social factors may also contribute to methods of control over youth behavior.

However, will the methods used in controlling youth behavior be effective in the presence of violence? Hirschi fails to address this issue in his theory of social control. Instead of focusing on the role of socialization, Hirschi seems to focus his argument more on the deviance that results when youths' social bonds are weak or broken. He seems to be discussing what did not happen versus the actual process involved in socialization that serves a preventive effect on youth criminal behavior. Social bonds theory is not a true theory of prevention. Although great amounts of empirical data exist to support social bonds theory, Hirschi's theory tends to fail to describe the chain of events necessary to prevent youth criminal behavior.

Self-Control Theory

Gottfredson and Hirschi's "general theory of crime" (i.e., self-control theory) helps to fill the gap in describing socialization processes that prevent youth criminal behavior. Socialization during childhood is the main contribution to youth crime under self-control theory: children are either trained or not trained to self-regulate their behavior. This training occurs primarily through the family, and more specifically the parents. The theory poses that self-control is the degree to which youth are prevented from engaging in criminal behavior, with some youth more vulnerable to acting out their criminal behavior compared to other youth. This level of vulnerability depends on whether or not youth had effective or ineffective socialization.

The key components of self-control theory are often referred to as the parental socialization thesis (Beaver, 2011; Beaver Ferguson, & Lynn-Whaley, 2010; Boyd & Higgins, 2006; De Li, 2004). This parental socialization thesis of self-control theory indicates that proper socialization includes actions parents need to take: children must be supervised, deviant behavior (i.e., youths' rule violations) must be recognized, and parents must immediately correct (i.e., discipline) the deviant behavior observed in children. When these conditions are met, youths' self-control remains constant throughout life (i.e., the stability thesis) and prevents crime. And the opposite is also argued in self-control theory: failure to properly socialize youth leads toward a lack of self-control and ultimately criminal behavior.

The current research demonstrates the efficacy of self-control theory in explaining the impact of familial socialization processes on preventing criminal behavior (e.g., Boyd & Higgins, 2006; Gibbs, Giever, & Martin, 1998; Johnson et al., 2011; Piquero & Bouffard, 2007). But there are several issues with Gottfredson and Hirschi's version of a social control theory. First, the parental socialization thesis discusses, in part, recognition of (Gottfredson & Hirschi, 1990) and punishment for deviant behavior (Gibbs, Giever, & Martin, 1998). Self-control theory appears to differentiate dysfunctional child-rearing practices from a more "normative," yet superficial, method. Gottfredson and Hirschi argue that parents must exert "adequate control" (1990, p. 96) over children's behavior to instill the ability for youth to self-regulate their own behavior. This control is advanced through socialization processes.

Gottfredson and Hirschi do not fully conceptualize "socialization." They fail to discuss in detail effective socialization compared to ineffective socialization used in the process to inculcate self-control. While Gottfredson and Hirschi indicate that "too harsh" punishment may not effectively control youth behavior (1990, pp. 100–101), there is no further discussion of the factors that contribute to youths' failure to develop self-control and prevent their criminal behavior. And, Gottfredson and Hirschi do not specifically define what constitutes harsh punishments or other components of ineffective socialization processes within either the original self-control theory (1990) or the revised self-control theory (Gottfredson, 2005; Hirschi, 2004).

Further, Gottfredson and Hirschi do not account for the variation of socialization processes transnationally. Gottfredson and Hirschi argue self-control theory can be applied cross-culturally and trans-nationally: crime is merely an act of achieving maximum pleasure at minimal cost in which the individual lacks self-regulation, and these basic principles are reflective in all societies. They argue that "important correlates of crime do not vary across cultures" (1990, p. 178). The argument later becomes correlates of criminal behavior may occur within a context, that "the behavior of individuals is a function of the strength of 'societies' " (Hirschi, 2004, p. 540). Such context may vary from nation to nation. Youth are socialized into society not only through their family but the standards in which the nation establishes for expectations of behavior. Therefore, under this argument, norms within a nation would not contribute to criminal behavior. Gottfredson and Hirschi make a contradictory argument.

Culture is an important aspect when exploring theories of crime involving socialization processes. Yet norms are one of the most important aspects of culture. Gottfredson and Hirschi's argument is that norms[2] "are *not* important in the causation of crime" (1990, p. 175 [emphasis in original]). This argument also fails to account for the influence of larger cultural norms that shape how families socialize youth, as well as consider that the family alone cannot account for *all* socialization of youth. Where did the family discern the standards for child-rearing and proper socialization of their children? What is the context in which socialization occurs in nations? There is no consideration for uniqueness in definitions of normative behavior transnationally within self-control theory. Gottfredson and Hirschi's (1990) contention that correlates of criminal behavior are invariant across different societies neglects cultural variation in norms, particularly concerning violence. Gottfredson and Hirschi make a convincing argument of self-control theory, but these points negate self-control theory as the single, universal criminological theory.

Not only do family systems have unique perspectives of "normal" behavior, but there are also cultural considerations that may impact socialization processes. As one example of cultural considerations within socialization processes, Annette Lareau (2002) conducted a longitudinal qualitative study of the culture of childhood socialization for middle-class, working-class, and poor families in Western Pennsylvania. Lareau discovered two unique socialization methods specific to parents' socioeconomic class: concerted cultivation for middle-class parents and accomplishment of natural growth for working-class and poor parents. Concerted cultivation is the constant engagement of children in planned recreational activities, in which children are closely supervised by adults. The accomplishment of natural growth focuses on autonomous play, in which children are left unsupervised to discover their own recreation. The socialization practices illustrated by Lareau were not individual decisions, or marked by individual influences. Rather, entire communities of families consistently engaged in these practices, from inner cities to rural lower socioeconomic groups.

Culturally accepted forms of socialization do not produce *all* the criminal elements of society. Yet Gottfredson and Hirschi would argue that the accomplishment of natural growth is the reason youth lack self-control, as these youth are not supervised. There are many middle-class youth, raised under concerted cultivation, who also engage in criminal behavior. If Gottfredson and Hirschi are unequivocally correct about the correlation between socialization and crime, then all criminals would originate in the lower classes under Lareau's model. Yet this simply is not the case. Youth criminal behavior is not exclusive among youth from lower-class socioeconomic status. And there is no direct correlation between socioeconomic status and delinquency rates (Tittle & Meier, 1990). Gottfredson and Hirschi fail to recognize cultural influences in socialization processes and the impact cultural influences have over youth behavior. This omission does not allow self-control theory to fully explore the association between socialization processes and criminal behavior.

There are still issues with the theory in explaining the link between socialization processes and criminal behavior. Gottfredson and Hirschi argue that other types of control are unimportant once a level of self-control is established within youth. The main argument of self-control theory seems to support the individual alone is responsible for engaging in criminal behavior, due to the individual's lack of self-control. Research indicates this may not be an accurate assessment. One study found that, although there was no strong evidence for higher levels of parental management directly decreasing juvenile deviant involvement, self-control mediated the relationship between parental management and deviant involvement (Gibbs, Giever, & Martin, 1998). In other words, higher levels of control exerted by parents contributed to higher levels of youth's self-control and a level of self-control decreased juvenile involvement in deviance. This demonstrates the importance of socialization processes: youth do not develop internal controls without the presence of external control. Thus, both types of social control are intricately link and equally important for helping to prevent youth criminal behavior.

Social Bonds/ Self-Control

To account for some of these discrepancies in their theory, Gottfredson and Hirschi re-conceptualized their control theories into a model of social bonds and self-control (*cf.* (Gottfredson, 2005; Hirschi, 2004). This version of control theory argues that attachments to children assist parents with recognizing and disciplining deviant behavior. The core thesis they argue involves two connected processes associated with control over youth behavior: the inculcation of self-control and attachments (*cf.* Hirschi, 2004). The parental socialization thesis now also discusses bonding with youth to inculcate consideration toward others (Gottfredson, 2005; Hirschi, 2004; Piquero & Bouffard, 2007). Attachments and discipline are methods of control parents exert over youth behavior (Beaver, Wright, & Delisi, 2007). According to this revised theory, these are two important dimensions of familial socialization processes used to control youth's behavior (see e.g., Boyd & Higgins, 2006; De Li, 2004; Johnson, Giordano, Manning, & Longmore, 2011).

In the more recent argument on parental discipline, Gottfredson (2005) and Hirschi (2004) now argue that youth will engage in criminal behavior if there are no restraints present to prevent such behavior. What if restraints are present, based on the normative standards of society, but youth criminal behavior persists despite such restraints? Might the family reproduce societal conditions reflected as normative? For example, norms within a nation may include adherence to the law, while at the same time promoting violent methods of control. Parents and other adult community members may encourage youth to use violent behavior in response to someone else using violent behavior. The justification for this advice is that the youth is merely defending themselves. The adults can further justify their pro-violent advice because that is the cultural norm in which they were socialized. The laws of a nation in which this scenario occurs may support a Lex Talonis approach to social control (e.g., capital punishment). Perhaps the use of violence within this scenario equates to "self-defense" and is supported in the laws of the nation. The collective members of society, in conjunction with the structure of society, create a national culture in which violence is a normative standard for controlling behaviors. The restraints over behavior are present, and youth become inculcated into a culture that justifies this use of violence. Yet Gottfredson and Hirschi did not foresee such life circumstances in their conceptualization of social bonds/self-control theory.

Since characteristics that occur at a higher level (i.e., structural factors) can influence individual-level characteristics (Luke, 2004), perhaps Gottfredson and Hirschi exaggerated a bit in their discussions of self-control when they make claims of generalization across all nations. As argued elsewhere (Kobayashi, et al., 2010), it cannot be assumed that the revised self-control theory can be generalized across all nations. Yet there appear to be no published studies that specifically examine an association between socialization processes and criminal behavior across different nations. This seems particularly important because Gottfredson argues that "a general cause should explain crime in different cultural settings" (2005, p. 84), yet current research is beginning to demonstrate that norms of violence could influence socialization processes within specific nations to be violent.

Even with a re-conceptualization of self-control theory, there is need to explore the association between violent socialization processes and criminal behavior. Gottfredson himself discusses the need to "constantly question" theories of crime, including self-control theory, in order to remain consistent with current literature (2005, p. 78). This literature indicates that self-regulation results from specific familial socialization processes (Buker, 2011). The opposite can be inferred: ineffective socialization processes may fail to inculcate self-regulation among youth. But what are these ineffective socialization processes?

What is the Direction for Social Control Theories?

Tests of social control theories have consistently identified a number of variables interdependently associated with socialization and youth criminal behavior. Attachments within the family are formed through the socialization process (e.g., Bowlby, 1969; Bowlby, 1973), and these attachments prevent youth criminal behavior (e.g., Barnes et al., 2006; Bjarnason, Thorlindsson, Sigfusdottir, & Welch, 2005; Bui, 2009; Goetting, 1994; Herrenkohl, Huang, Tajima, & Whitney, 2003; Luthar & Goldstein, 2008; Matherne & Thomas, 2001; Parker & Benson, 2004; Turner, Hartman, & Bishop, 2007). The inculcation of self-control is another aspect of socialization process associated with the prevention of youth criminal behavior (e.g., Gibson, Morris, & Beaver, 2009; Grasmick, Tittle, Bursik, & Arneklev, 1993; Piquero & Bouffard, 2007; Rebellon, Straus, & Medeiros, 2008). Thus, attachments for youth and the ability to develop self-control are crucial aspects of preventing youth criminal behavior. However, socialization processes encompass more than just bonds and self-regulation. Examining specific methods used to control youth behavior is necessary. For example, physical abuse, in combination with low parent-child bonding, significantly increases the risk of criminal behavior (Teague, Mazerolle, Legosz, & Sanderson, 2008). Social control theories need to take an approach that considers the extent to which overly punitive social control contributes to youth criminal behavior. Such punitive control includes violent socialization processes.

Culture-Based Theories

Culture-based theories help to explain how youth are socialized into a culture and this socialization contributes to their criminal behavior. Some theories focus on micro-level crime, while others consider macro-level crime. But all theories focus on particular groups of people and their culture. Norms are represented through group culture, in which customs and values guide behavior for members of the group. This culture is transmitted through social actions of members of the group to new generations of group members. This cultural transmission reinforces and reproduces the group norms. These theories seem to argue that successful criminals become role models for youth, demonstrating the normality of criminal behavior. The group then strengthens its norms by exercising social pressure for youth to engage in criminal behavior.

Anomie Theories

Anomie theories are macro-level theories that explain variation in crime rates via culture. Robert Merton originated these theories to explain crime, at the macro-level, in society. Merton (1938) argues that the cultural-social structure explains crime, insofar as culture becomes the motivation for crime. Specifically, the distribution of resources across society and the desire for monetary success (material worth) has such significant symbolic value within American culture that members of society, collectively, engage in crime to achieve the "dream." Crime, then, is motivational because members of society do not have the means for financial success, as culture dictates are symbolic of success within American culture. This disconnect between values and means, in which cultural values outweigh legitimate means, creates anomie, and it is this anomie that creates crime in American society. Other anomie-based theories have a similar basic argument (e.g., Institutional Anomie Theory [see Messner & Rosenfeld, 2008]).

Anomie theories are not as well supported in the current criminological literature (Curran & Renzetti, 1994). This is most likely because the main argument of the theories focuses on a specific structure of one nation (United States) and there is no true transnational comparison. The theories propel a motivation to explain why crime happens from a socioeconomic position. The argument takes a limited perspective in which crime is more difficult to avoid because groups of people lack both financial and social capital necessary to achieve success. There is no consideration for individual actions, choices, or behaviors. There is no in-depth consideration for motivations outside economics.

Anomie theories tend to be mostly a comparison of American culture to other nations to explain high crime rates in the United States. Thus, these theories are not fully transnational explanations for youth criminal behavior. Further, the focus of the theories is on crime rates rather than criminal behavior. These theories do not address individual-level processes nor criminal behavior.

And, while these theories address structural issues within a nation contributing to crime, anomie theories take a singular focus on culture: monetary issues. There is little consideration for the other components of culture (e.g., norms). Anomie theory is distinct from sub-cultural theories, in that anomie argues that pressures form from marginalization in society, and these pressures (anomie) lead toward crime. Subculture theories also discuss pressure from culture, but focus more on learning the culture within a given area and how this regionally-based culture is so pervasive that individuals need to adapt to the culture (i.e., criminal behavior varies within given areas).

Sub-Cultural Theories

This paradigm of criminological theories argues that the cultural structure of groups within society holds values and attitudes that are conducive to crime and violence. The norms within society may not be reflective in these groups. Instead, these groups tend to have distinctive norms differing from mainstream culture. These differences may not necessarily represent a culture deviant of the majority of society. Rather, the groups have developed a subculture that contributes to youth criminal behavior.

The focus of these theories is often on isolated locations or groups rather than a general theory across space and people. Some theorists focus their thesis on specific areas of violence within the United States (e.g., Southern Culture of Violence [*cf.* Wolfgang & Ferratucci, 1967]). Other theorists claim that crime occurs because of a specific location, such as urban area (e.g., see Fischer, 1995; Shaw, 1930[1966]). But, most cultural theorists claim that crime occurs within specific groups with particular characteristics. These characteristics include, for example being a member of a gang, having a lower socioeconomic status, being male, and being of a particular age group (i.e., youth).

Cohen (1955) focused on all these factors when he studied the lifestyles of adolescent, working-class-male youth within impoverished urban locations. The argument of this socioeconomic based theory was that some youth engage in criminal behavior due to characteristics of their lower-class status. The research found that these young male gang members formed a subculture of crime to rebel against the middle class because they lacked economic and social opportunity within mainstream society (Cohen & Short, 1958). Cloward and Ohlin ([1960]2001) and Miller (1998) take a more strict socioeconomic status approach focusing exclusively on a subculture of the lower class. However, their research sampled male youth exclusively, essentially mimicking previous research.

Subcultural theories of crime tend to focus on geographical arguments. The theories discuss crime occurring within a limited geographical area. Wolfgang and Ferracuti (1967) argue that the reason for higher incidents of violence is a subculture of violence within the southern portion of the United States. Despite their argument that there is a distinctive subculture in the South, with values, attitudes, and social expectations specific to this geographical region, the focus, again, is on lower social class. Violence is reinforced in everyday interactions of the less economically advantaged in society (Lee, & Ousey, 2012). The argument continues that only lower-class groups find violence acceptable, which is transmitted to younger generations only within the lower class. The theory, using homicide rates, argues that people born in the southern parts of America have been socialized into a set of values that condone violence interaction (Ousey & Lee, 2010). The issue is that crime is limited to homicide rates. Certainly, homicide does not represent all criminal behavior (see LaFree, 2005). And, these theories fail to account for homicide rates transnationally.

Many subcultural theories of crime take the position that violence is deviant invariantly. This is reinforced by the argument that violence must be justified for use and only allowable in certain situations (*cf.* Wolfgang & Ferracuti, 1967). Within the limited groups for which subcultural theories address, the norm seems to be that violence is appropriate for dealing with conflict. A common argument of culture of violence theories is that individuals who use violence have "overcome normative boundaries" that prohibit violence (Alvarez & Bachman, 2017, p. 4). There seems to be little account for other norms, particularly when these norms are tolerant of violence. The main argument seems to be that violence as an acceptable method of dispute resolution would be unacceptable for other groups within society.

Moving Culture-Based Theories Forward

Culture of violence theories fails to discuss the latent manifestations of covert violence. This is the violence that is so habituated within the structural culture of a society that the actions are not viewed as violent. This concept is particularly relevant to violence as an instrument for social control. For example, the use of physical punishment on children is not seen as violence, but rather an accepted method to control children's behavior (Gagné, et al., 2007; Socolar & Stein, 1995). Yet hitting other people in any other context is considered violence. There is variation in the use of physical discipline, and this variation tends to occur at the individual level (families). At the structural level, violence has been state sanctioned as social control. For example, the use of capital punishment (i.e., the death penalty) is acceptable in some nations. Yet homicide is a crime and considered a grave violation of social norms. Violence, then, is an expected behavior. Yet violence may be so inure within families, communities, and the structure of a nation that certain actions may not actually be considered violence. These contradictory positions indicate that variation exists in the norms of different nations. But the current prominent culture of violent theories fail to discuss this variation.

This raises another issue with culture of violence theories: the divergence of the macro- and micro-levels to explain culture. Some theories address criminal behavior within smaller groups (the micro- or meso-level), while other theories address crime rates (macro-level). Culture and crime are not limited to specific groups or locations. All members of a nation, including the families and communities nested within those nations, are socialized into the culture of the nation. This includes norms. Norms occur at all levels of society: families at the micro-level, communities at the meso-to-macro levels, and national structure at the macro-level. There may very well be subtle differences regionally or by group within a specific nation. But as a whole, subtle differences are inconsequential to the greater context of culture within societies. Violence may occur *de facto* within nations. It is the shared collective behaviors of a nation, based on the totality of norms within a nation, that determine culture (*cf.* Durkheim, 1977 [1914]). Violence that occurs at the societal level may impact the communities and the families that live in those communities. Rather than asking why individuals commit crime, which seems to be the main question of culture-based theories, the question needs to be extended to what social forces within a nation constitute norms that support violence.

The argument could be made that culture-based theories fail to adequately address the origins of violence. Culture of violence theories need to explain where this violence comes from. There are some limited arguments about the origins of culture of violence. There are inferences that the origins of culturally accepted violence occur in the realms of politics (e.g., slavery), ethnicity (e.g., herding communities), and religion (see Lee & Ousey, 2012, for a review). All these speculations are based in arguments of social control. And, there is little research to support these contentions (Curran & Renzetti, 1994). The other argument is that violence tolerance is part of the socialization processes. This renders culture-based theories as either a social control theory or learning theory.

Learning Theory

Learning theories are micro-level theories that explain why youth engage in criminal behavior: they learn it. All theories contain some aspect of social psychological argument that behavior is learned through observation, imitation, and modeling. Bandura (1977) argues that after watching others' behaviors (observation) and copying those behaviors (imitation), children and youth then begin to model those same behaviors over time after repetitive exposure. This includes criminal behavior. The family is one of the foci of learning theories. Youth may learn unacceptable behavior by mimicking their parents repeatedly (Ormrod, 1999), including the modeling of discipline during play (Midlarsky, Bryan, & Brickman, 1973).

Another focus of learning theories is peers. The association with deviant peers exposes individuals to an environment in which they learn to engage in criminal behavior. These deviant individuals expose the individual to a social environment with varying definitions of acceptable and unacceptable behaviors, and those environments in which crime is favorable will lead the individual to engage in criminal behavior (Sutherland, 1974). It is the extent of this exposure which determines why some individuals learn to commit crime. These theories argue that this level of exposure, both in terms of physical presence and group attitudes, reinforces the learning of criminal behavior and youth then act out the same criminal behavior.

According to some social learning theories, these learned behaviors are then either positively reinforced (i.e., rewards) or negatively punished (i.e., sanctions), motivating future engagement in or avoidance of the learned behaviors (Akers, 2009). Motivation tends to be a key argument of learning theories: youth are motivated to commit crime. For example, the self-determinate theory argues that youth tend to be motivated to learn to behave in effective and healthy ways, including self-regulation over their own behavior (Ryan & Deci, 2000). But, learning theories do not take into consideration the concept of emergence. There is no discussion of collective behaviors or how these group behaviors are formed. Yet nations contain some degree of collective behaviors. Otherwise, there would be no norms within a nation. The "collective phenomenon" within a nation is "collaboratively created by individuals" within that nation and "not reducible to individual action" (Sawyer, 2001). The basis of social learning theories is that learning occurs within a social context (Ormrod, 1999), and this context is the environment surrounding the individual. The environment may lead people to behave in certain ways, but the context in reference simply suggests individuals learn from one another. There is not sufficient elaboration beyond this combination of the environmental and personal psychological factors that determine youth criminal behavior.

Social learning theories are based mostly on an individual's contact with other youth who engage in criminal behavior resulting in a "criminal education." More explanations of why youth criminal behavior occurs are redundant—youth teach other youth to commit crimes. A new theoretical approach is needed to explain variation in youth crime across different nations. And this approach incorporates the necessity of socialization to prevent youth criminal behavior without the "modeling" of that behavior. Not all socialization involves modeled behavior. Norms can be transmitted through formal means, such as laws. Norms can also be transmitted through replication of repeated social interactions within social institutions, such as familial socialization processes. There are wide-ranging methods used to inculcate youth into the norms of a nation. Certain behaviors are accepted simply as a normative standard within society. This includes some aspects of violence.

Violent Socialization and Criminological Theory

Some may argue that social control theories simply reflect learning. Within the socialization process, some observation may occur, as all of life involves some degree of observation. To inculcate control within youth, youth need not mimic the behaviors they observe. Nor do youth need to emulate that behavior. Instead, socialization is the manner in which youth are trained to conform to the norms of society, regardless of whether or not youth mimic observed behavior. Socialization infiltrates multiple spheres of social life, and is not limited to the individual. These multiple spheres establish a standard. And norms, as collective processes within society, are integral to socialization processes.

From a social control theory perspective, violent socialization processes are not the equivalent of teaching youth deviant behaviors or youth learning violent behavior. Violent socialization processes are the absence of effective socialization by the family. Learning theories argue that youth learn to be violent from observing their family engage in violent behavior then modeling this behavior (*cf.* Bandura, 1977). Youth may learn unacceptable behavior by mimicking their parents then modeling during play (Midlarsky, Bryan, & Brickman, 1973). But even if youth learn criminal behavior, their behavior must be controlled. Control is not always rewards and punishments. Rather control can be achieved through conformity to societal norms. If these norms include a pro-violent stance, then the normative standard supports violence. Youth who are consistently exposed to violence within their family may be socialized by parents who lack control over their own behavior. The argument is not that exposure to violence is a sort of modeling process that teaches youth to be violent. Rather, the failure of parents to recognize deviant behavior (*cf.* Gottfredson & Hirschi, 1990), in terms of violence, may contribute to the inadequate development of self-control within youth. Socialization must include recognition that violence is wrong. This is not learning.

Discipline, according to self-control theory, is a familial socialization process intended to instill in youth the ability to self-regulate their behavior (Gottfredson & Hirschi, 1990). The argument is that discipline is necessary to correct and control undesirable behavior, not necessarily to model socially approved behavior for children. Violent discipline, in conjunction with the failure to recognize deviant behavior due to other dimensions of violent socialization processes, may be ineffective at controlling youth behavior. Violent socialization processes establish a standard of accepting violent methods of social control at a macro- and micro-levels rather than specifically targeting individuals to teach them violence. Society itself is instilling the normative standard of violence and reinforcing this norm. It is the use of control at an aggregate level, not the individual process of one's psyche.

Where Do We Go from Here?

None of these theories alone adequately explains the context for the development of youth criminal behavior. Theories of youth crime reference some of the dimensions of violent socialization, but fail to fully discuss all three dimensions of violent familial socialization processes. Instead, an integrated approach to explaining the foundation or the context that influences youth criminal behavior is necessary. Overall, social control theories argue that there is a defective socialization process that prevents youth from developing control over their criminal behavior. Cultural theories explain youth crime as values that differ from societal mainstream norms. The premise of this book is a quantitative test of an *integrated* theory of social control and culture of violence. The focus is not solely on the theoretical propositions of one specific theory. This newly proposed theory begins to explain variation in youth criminal behavior across different nations from the stance of social control within a national structure that endorses violence.

The focus is more on the origins of youth criminal behavior, not explanations for the variance throughout the life course, individual reactions and attitudes, or influence of others in learning crime. All these origins are based in socialization processes. Socialization involves, to some extent, distinct actions. Such actions are better measures associated with criminal behavior than youth's attitudes or youth's prior behavior (Morris, Gerber, & Menard, 2011). The theory is looking at the course toward criminal behavior through socialization processes: the actions engaged with the intention to inculcate youth into the norms of society and control youth behavior yet are ineffective due to the manifestation of violence as a normative method for social control. This is a transnational comparative study, exploring the degree to which there is variation across different nations. Studying the association between violent socialization processes and criminal behavior is instrumental to understand the extent to which some socialization processes, such as violent socialization processes, fail to prevent criminal behavior.

Another difference between control theories and the proposed new theory is social control theories seem to take a bifurcated approach to control: it is either direct control or indirect control. Socialization is a form of direct control: established norms transmitted to youth, and informal sanctions for youth who violate those norms. The purpose of socialization is to instill a sense of self-restraint and regulation. But what if, through the processes of socialization, there is a failure to inculcate this restraint and control because socialization processes are advance violence in a normative fashion? What is the effect of normative violence-based sanctions on youths' criminal behavior? What happens when youth are socialized into nations in which violence is a norm?

Criminological theories have failed to specify the contexts in which violence occurs across and within different nations beyond a sub-cultural approach. One reason may be that many theories take on a binary approach to explaining violence and youth criminal behavior. The focus is either micro-level explanations for individuals or small groups, or strictly macro-level structural explanations. Current theories of crime fail to acknowledge the contribution of macro-level influences spilling over into micro-level processes. This book sets forth support for an integrated theory that encompasses the premises of social control within a culture of violence. This newly proposed theoretical perspective is not postulating culture-based explanations for criminal behavior. Subcultural theories of crime imply that criminal behavior is reserved to a subset of the population, rather than recognize that criminal behavior varies both among individuals within a nation and across different nations. Instead, the theory integrates a social control approach that every youth is susceptible to criminal behavior and preventative measures are necessary, while recognizing a culture of societal endorsed violence renders these prevention efforts ineffective. And this newly proposed thesis addressed the cross-level effects of the macro spilling over into the micro.

Notes

1 The age aspect is particularly important because young children are not seen as "rational beings" and need proper "training" to control their behavior.

2 In their original conceptualization of self-control theory, Gottfredson and Hirschi (1990) use the word "culture" and "cultural variability" to refer to nations and norms within a nation.

Chapter 3

Norms of Violence

Theories of crime take a bifurcated perspective when trying to explain the contributing factors of youth criminal behavior. Criminological theories waver between a structural/cultural approach and individual "causes" of criminal behavior (Case, 2008). This type of "either/or" approach limits the ability of the theory to offer full consideration of the totality of conditions that influence youth criminal behavior. Among the plethora of theories, few offer consistent empirical validity to support the contentions. As parsimonious as some of the theories present, many of the existing theories simply cannot be tested to demonstrate empirical validity. The theories with the strongest consistent empirical theory were presented in Chapter 2. These theories offer compelling support. Yet the theories are still fallible when trying to explain youth criminal behavior across different nations. And, most of these theories fail to account for the link between youth victimization and youth criminal behavior. As argued previously, these theories lack scope transnationally. A new, integrated approach is necessary to examine factors contributing to youth crime, one that incorporates the victimization-criminal behavior link.

Violent Socialization as Victimization

Violence endorsed by society is supported in both the structure and the day-to-day practices for members of a nation. The focus in the study of violence tends to be large scale, overt acts or conditions. Yet much violence is obscure. Of the obscure constructs of violence in society, there are some more obvious manifestations of covert violence. Socialization processes embedded in violence are a latent manifestation of covert violence. These processes are multiple dimensions of violence that occur as part of the socialization of youth that are collectively sub-conscious within some nations. And these violent socialization processes have consequences.

Child maltreatment is a serious social issue (Finkelhor & Wells, 2003) that remains mostly hidden from society. Such maltreatment remains hidden due to the covert nature of most violence within societies. For example, violent socialization processes are embedded within society to the degree that these processes are not recognized as violence within some nations. These socialization processes are conducted repetitively without mindfulness to the violence these actions entail. The repetitive exposure to violence is one embodiment of child maltreatment. Experiences with violent socialization, particularly if sustained within both families and communities, may be the most repetitive of violence within a nation. Violent methods for socializing youth could, arguably, contribute to the defective upbringing of youth. The consistent transmission and reinforcement of normalized violence, particularly in the face of conflict, can damage youth's mental state. Over time, this normalized violence could produce varying levels of trauma, creating trauma-based reactions.

One of the external manifestations of the damage suffered by youth is reckless, antisocial behaviors (Kerig, 2019; Widom & Maxfield, 2001). Research over the past several decades have demonstrated that child maltreatment contributes to negative effects on the developmental process of children (Petersen, Joseph, & Feit, 2014). Youth exposed to violent socialization processes, first within their families and then reinforced within communities in their nations, simply may not be able to integrate a healthy level of self-control over their behaviors. Instead, youth act out externally. The Diagnostic and Statistical Manual of Mental Disorders includes risky behavior as a symptom of post-traumatic stress disorder (American Psychiatric Association, 2013). Risky behavior includes criminal behavior. It is well documented that experiences with child victimization, including violence, are associated with youth criminal behavior (see Jung, Herrenkohl, Lee, Hemphill, Heerde, & Skinner, 2017 for a review of the literature). And much research supports the link between trauma and youth criminal behavior (see Kerig, 2019 for a different review). The consequences of violence exposure is not surprising: trauma leading toward increased youth criminal behavior. The victimization effect of violent socialization processes creates a culture of trauma for youth.

But the victimizing effect may not be solely culturally based. Exposure to violence also includes actively telling youth to engage in violence to resolve conflict. Such pro-violent advice can contribute to criminal behavior. Parents or other adult authority figures in the community who counsel children to respond to violence with violence are, theoretically, contributing to the possibility of youth internalizing conflict resolution positions favoring criminal behavior (i.e., assault is an appropriate means to resolve conflict). Research supports this contention. Childhood victimization has been shown to impact behavior within intimate dating relationships, including acting out violently (Abbey, Parkhill, BeShears, Clinton-Sherrod, & Zawacki, 2006; DeGue, DiLillo, & Scalora, 2010; Feder, Levant, & Dean, 2010; Forbes & Adams-Curtis, 2001; Kahn & Paluzzi, 2006; Margolin & Gordis, 2000; Mattingly & Straus, 2008; Milletich, Kelley, Doane, & Pearson, 2010; Spano, Rivera, & Bolland, 2010). Therefore, it is not only direct exposure to violence that contributes to this victimizing effect, but also being advised to engage in violence.

One of the better researched aspects of violent socialization processes is the use of physical discipline on children. There has been an ongoing debate, transnationally, about the impact of using physical discipline to correct children's behavior. Many people may not consider the acts of hitting a child to be a manifestation of violence. Yet there remains a "fine line between legitimate and illegitimate acts" (Miller-Perrin & Perrin, 1999, p. 20) when disciplining of a child. Violence becomes a form of justice when used as punishment, retaliation, or revenge (Black, 2004). However, this does not diminish the act as violence. Striking a child is more an emotional reaction to an unwanted behavior as opposed to socializing children into acceptable behavior. The occasional physical punishment may not be viewed as child maltreatment, but rather a family "problem." Family problems often do not constitute child maltreatment. Such "problems" may be indicators of family *dysfunction*. Can this "dysfunction" contribute to the victimizing effect? The research outlined previously indicates the answer is yes.

The argument seems to be "but they are children." What is the difference between hitting a child and hitting an adult? The only difference is, in essence, age. Hitting a person, regardless of their age, is still hitting another person. In this instance, the answer gravitates more toward control. This argument is no different from an abusive person hitting their intimate partner to control behavior. These are both methods of external control that utilize violence, yet one manifestation is more culturally acceptable than the other in some nations. Physical discipline of a child, even if used to control youth behavior, may actually be a form of victimization. But physical discipline alone is not adequate to explain the victimizing nature of violent socialization processes and consequences of such victimization. There are other aspects of violent socialization processes.

The currently published literature tends to neglect these multiple dimensions of violent socialization as ineffective methods to control youth behavior because these methods victimize children. Yet, the literature separates such dimensions into singular categories as if the processes of socialization occur in isolation from other processes. And, childhood victimizing experiences from violence transcend from multiple domains in their life. This includes the family, the community, and the structure of a nation. The norms established within these domains impact the well-being of children (Smagur, Bogat, & Leveondosky, 2017). The theoretical proposition presented in this book expands upon the current literature by examining the *multiple* dimensions of violent socialization processes, across different domains of a nation that *together* contribute to the victimization of youth and fail to control youth criminal behavior.

Violent Socialization and Youth Criminal Behavior

The causes of criminal behavior are diverse and complex (Church, Wharton, & Taylor, 2009; Edwards, 1996). Ineffective socialization fails to control youth aggression (Cooper, Masi, & Vick, 2009). The failure of parents to effectively control youth's behavior could lead to criminal behavior (*cf.* Gottfredson & Hirschi, 1990). What about control exerted by means other than parents? Socialization supports the existing social structure of a nation by maintaining social order. This social order involves both external and internal controls, and socialization serves to establish both these controls. The expectations placed on youth by the community and structure of a nation are external controls. If external controls are effective, youth develop internal controls that regulate their behavior. Socialization processes, then, are connected to youth behavior. These arguments can be extended to control over youth criminal behavior. Youth criminal behavior may be exasperated if the socialization processes occur within contexts of violence.

Violent Socialization and Social Control

Socialization processes in and of itself is a form of social control. Social control is necessary to ensure youth do not deviate from norms. Violent socialization processes have this same goal of preventing youth-deviant behaviors, including crime. From a control perspective, then, violent socialization does not provide a model of deviance or actively promotes deviance. Instead, violent socialization involves external methods attempting to control youth's behavior but may ultimately be ineffective in promoting control among youth.

It has been argued elsewhere that ineffective socialization processes are one of the best predictors associated with involvement in criminal behavior (Loeber & Dishion, 1983). Socialization processes that are overly punitive, and do not provide comfort or care toward youth, may contribute to youth's inability to self-regulate their criminal behavior (Wright & Cullen, 2001). Therefore, some socialization processes are counterproductive. Violent socialization processes may be one example. The violence within socialization processes may have a dual impact: failure to prevent youth criminal behavior and instill the ability of youth to control their criminal behavior.

Family

Families provide varying levels of control over youth behavior (Brown & Rinelli, 2010). These methods of control can be conceptualized as familial socialization processes. It is the degree to which parents exert "adequate control" (Gottfredson & Hirschi, 1990, p. 96) over youth's behavior that instills the ability for youth to self-regulate their own behavior. But not all familial socialization processes offer equal control over youth behavior. It is a combination of systemic dysfunction in the family that best predicts criminal behavior (Dillon, Pantin, Robbins, & Szapocznik, 2008; Dufour, Clément, Chamberland, & Dubeau, 2011). Certain parental "acts," engaged under the auspices of social control, may constitute risk factors for youth criminal behavior (Hirschi, 2004;

Loeber & Stouthamer-Loeber, 1986; Rutter, Quinton, & Hill, 1990). Such acts include violent socialization processes. And these acts occur simultaneously within the totality of the socialization process for children.

Research has consistently demonstrated that socialization processes within individual families are associated with criminal behavior (Goddard, Goff, Melancon, & Huebner, 2000). Youth will engage in criminal behavior if there are no restraints present to prevent such behavior (Gottfredson, 2005). What if restraints are present within the family, but such restraints are ineffective at controlling criminal behavior? Violent familial socialization processes are one such restraint. The intention of the familial socialization processes is to control youth behavior. Yet the meaning conveyed to youth is that violence is an acceptable method of conflict resolution. Such a mixed message may be confusing to youth, and instead inculcates youth into a normative standard in which some acts of violence become acceptable. Youth may then reproduce this violence through acting out in illicit ways within their communities. The criminal behavior among youth becomes reactionary to the violence experienced within their family.

Since "parental support and control have been found to be critically important in the family socialization/ parenting process" (Barnes, et al., 2006, p. 1085) and the family has a responsibility to instill a sense of personal limitations for unacceptable behavior (Kendall, 2010), some may argue that attachments within the family serve a preventative function. This is supported in the research which has found that poor parent–child interactions are associated with various types of criminal behavior (e.g. Goetting, 1994; Herrenkohl, Huang, Tajima, & Whitney, 2003; Johnson, et al., 2011). But attachments can occur within families that use violent methods of socialization. The family can be supportive of the youth, providing understanding to the youth and helping the youth with problems they experience.

At the same time, the family may be failing to support the development of self-control because parents support the use of violence, as demonstrated within the presence of violent socialization processes. A study empirically testing the effect of both attachments and self-control on criminal behavior found that while parental support was associated with less criminal behavior among youth, this relationship was diminished, to some extent, when accounting for the effects of violent discipline toward youth (Johnson et al., 2011). Although the measure of violent discipline (e.g., hitting or slapping the youth) in this study is not quite the same as violent familial socialization processes, these results might indicate that the attachments parents form with youth may not provide sufficient control over youth criminal behavior with violent familial socialization processes. Another study supports this contention. Physical abuse, in combination with low parent–child bonding, significantly increases the risk of criminal behavior (Teague, Mazerolle, Legosz, & Sanderson, 2008).

Criminal behavior can become the standard of behavior among youth from families with poor methods of socialization (Fonagy et al., 1997). This argument can be made for violent familial socialization processes. Even in the presence of protective factors, violent familial socialization processes may increase youth criminal behavior. The present study tests this hypothesis: *youth from families that use violent socialization processes will engage in more criminal behavior, compared to youth from families that do not use violent socialization processes even in the presence of effective social control markers* (H_1).

But is this micro-level explanation enough? Clearly not when trying to explain youth criminal behavior. Methods of control over youth behavior extend beyond the singular influence of familial socialization processes. Violence in the family is a reflection of violence within society (Wyatt, 1994), including violent familial socialization processes. Such obscure socialization processes occurring across many different families within the same nation may reinforce a context in which violence, in general, is supported. But the risk for criminal behavior among youth may not result exclusively from violent socialization within the youth's family. Normative experiences with violence may also stem from group-level processes of socialization. Each nation embraces different norms surrounding the acceptability of violence. And evidence of the acceptance of violent socialization lies in the expressive actions of members of the community.

Community

The social practices of aggregates of families within a given nation can constitute a context for the socialization of youth within that nation. Aggregates of families within the same nation may embrace similar methods of control over youth behavior and these methods coincide within a context of violence unique to that nation. For example, Forjuoh and Zwi (1998) argue that widespread *societal* views on discipline influence families' methods of control over youth behavior. Physical discipline is one method of familial socialization process that is part of a universal context within the same nation (Knowles, 1996). Hence, aggregates of families within the same nation may similarly engage in violent socialization processes. Violent familial socialization processes may not necessarily be isolated methods of control within each individual family but instead occur within a context specific to some nations. This context of violence includes violent disciplinary techniques occurring among aggregates of families across the same nation. When similar violent socialization processes occur across multiple different families within the same nation, context becomes a function of the norms for that nation.

Culture provides the framework for which members within a particular nation understand the expectations for social behavior and engage in that appropriate behavior. The culture of a nation offers the strategies necessary to navigate society (Swindler, 1986). Nations establish their culture through various macro-level indicators. For example, the law sets the norms for which individuals may act toward others. Corporal discipline is a form of violent touch, hitting, as a method of control parents use to deal with conflict that occurs with their children. In other words, when children engage in behavior that parents do not agree, the parent will use violence to address that unwanted behavior. While parents may treat their children as property and use violence to discipline their children, these same adults may be sanctioned for using violence on their actual property: pets. Adults may be formally sanctioned for violating animal anti-abuse laws when using corporal discipline on their pets. This equates children, vulnerable human life, to less than property. What message does this send within the culture of that nation? Violence is an acceptable means in which to deal with conflict.

The family is a part of society, and has no identity without also having the identity of the nation in which the family is an institution (*cf.* Mead, 1934). The "social exchange" between the family and greater society is part of an expected role performance and "may be roughly defined as the reciprocal influence of individuals upon one another's actions" (Goffman, 1959, p. 15). Aggregates of families reside in communities and must conform to the standards of these communities in order to be accepted within that community. In other words, families using violent socialization processes to control youth behavior are not acting independent of the communities in which they reside or the norms of the nation that define cultural practices. Violent socialization occurring among many different families within any given society might indicate a communal pattern within that nation.

In an analogous study exploring national context effects, national religiosity has been conceptualized as similar religious beliefs among groups of people within the same nation with these religious beliefs are strongly tied to a specific nation (Kelley & De Graaf, 1997). National religiosity was found to be a stronger influence on children's religious beliefs than individual parental socialization around religion (Kelley & De Graaf, 1997). This is an example of the aggregating effect of shared commonalities within a nation. Societal norms of violence may influence socialization processes over and above the methods of socialization used within individual families. This clustering effect needs to be considered.

Socialization as social control is part of a collective process, a context in which socialization occurs above and beyond the socialization of youth by their individual families (Pratt, Turner, & Piquero, 2004). Since communities are nested within nations, communities are also part of the socialization of youth. To be successful in a role performance normative to the nation, communities must also conform to the normative standards of a nation. Socialization processes serve to reinforce the normative standards of a society, albeit informally. Communities would then need to engage in common socialization processes in order to create an environment that leads youth to act voluntarily in their own expressive behaviors (Goffman, 1959) as well as reproduce the norms of society. Community is part of a greater context and this context influences the expressive behavior for members of the society.

Community-based violent socialization comprises acts reproducing the culture of violence within the nation, contributing to the normalization of violence within the nation's structure. These communities' actions are separate from, yet complementary to, the actions of the family. Violence may be so inculcated within the day-to-day functioning of any given nation that communities may not be aware of engaging in patterns of violence when socializing youth. Community-based violent socialization is also part of a contextual effect specific to the nation and can contribute to youth criminal behavior. This proposition will be tested under the following hypothesis: *youth in communities that use violent socialization processes will engage in more criminal behavior, compared to youth in communities that do not use violent socialization processes* (H_2).

Individual-level variables, such as the family and specific communities do not capture the full degree to which socialization processes may prevent criminal behavior (Morrongiello, Corbett, & Bellissimo, 2008). Micro- and meso-level factors alone cannot account for the conditions that contribute to youth criminal behavior. The community-based argument needs to be extended to the large-scale community: the nation. Over time, societal ideas for indicators of violence may be a slow evolution of norms. As these norms change over time, the norms may be reflected within the structure of a nation. Therefore, macro-level influences must also be considered.

Conditions of a Nation

Methods of social control have been conceptualized as connected processes (Hirschi, 2004; Vold, Bernard, & Snipes, 1998). The connected processes include both micro-level and macro-level factors. There are multiple different regulatory forces within a nation, including formal laws and informal social norms, which can shape the collective behaviors for aggregates of families and communities (Knowles, 1996). The family, which engages informal norms, is a micro-level factor. Each society establishes a "spectrum of acceptable behavior in family" through a "web of social practices" (Knowles, 1996, p. 33) used to control behavior. These webs include macro-level forces, such as laws. Multiple regulatory forces exist within any given nation that influence the methods used to socialize youth and control their behavior (Knowles, 1996). Thus, socialization processes transcend all these conditions within a nation.

LAWS

The laws of a nation can reflect the social climate of a nation. Laws are part of social processes that, over long periods of time, become part of the normative experiences within each nation. Laws can reflect the general social conditions within a nation. For example, around the late 1800s, the citizenry in Sweden began to question the social climate of the nation that allowed the use of physical discipline on children, leading to the first law in 1902 that legally prohibited the severe physical maltreatment of children (Janson, Långberg, & Svensson, 2011). While the debates on the use of physical discipline continued, Sweden officially banned the use of physical discipline on children within schools in 1957 (Janson, Långberg, & Svensson, 2011). With the citizenry continuing to view violence against children as non-normative over time, the law eventually prohibited the use of physical discipline within families in 1979 (Gumbrecht, 2011). Processes for creating laws that reflect the social conditions within a nation, in this instance Sweden, may take long periods of time in order to capture changes in norms within the nation. But, in general, nations may pass laws prohibiting the use of physical discipline on children because the general social conditions within the nation, over time, have evolved such that the majority of citizenry desire a social climate in which violence should not be a normative experience.

Laws can be important reflections of the overall norms within the nation. Law and policy are orientated toward common morals within a nation, binding the citizenry together (Sarat, 2001). Laws determine the formalized treatment of the members of a nation. Laws may even serve as a reflection of civility within a nation, such that Such laws focused on the most vulnerable members may be indicative of societal views towards vulnerable populations. Such laws include the use of corporal punishment on youth and the presence of capital punishment on those convicted of crimes.

Capital Punishment There is variation in sentencing for criminal offenses across nations, based on differences in laws. There are also divergences in both the conditions and operations of incarceration from nation to nation. These variances make measuring the treatment of prisoners transnationally nearly impossible. However, laws surrounding the use of capital punishment are relatively consistent. Whether or not a nation has a law abolishing the death penalty is either present or not present.

There has been international criticism toward nations that use capital punishment (Sarat, 2001). Capital punishment is perhaps the most severe form of social control. An argument can be made that capital punishment makes a victim out of criminal offenders, via state-sanctioned homicide. The justification is retribution for violation of social norms. Some have argued that capital punishment is state-sanctioned murder (Kain & Recinella, 2017), and others have argued that death penalty can be viewed as another social problem with society (Bohm, 2017). The opposition contends that severe punishment is necessarily not only to control behavior, but to serve justice to victims. Yet victims of crime, as well as members of society living in high crime areas, have less support for the use of capital punishment compared to other members of the nation (Cao, Lai, & Huang, 2020). And some nations have taken to prevent the use of capital punishment transnationally. For example, European nations have decreed a non-extradition of suspected criminals to America due to the use of capital punishment in this nation (Sarat, 2001). Despite these criticisms, capital punishment still exists including in progressive, democratic nations. The implication is that violence is acceptable within those nations bcause laws allowing the use of capital punishment.

State-sanctioned violent actions toward the most vulnerable of the population is another example of the culture supporting a norm of violence: the use of capital punishment on convicted law violators as a deterrent effect on members of a nation. Prisoners are subject to the will of the State, enacted through human beings hired to supervise the prisoners and enact the policies of the State. Capital punishment, then, reflects the norms of a nation. The research on capital punishment supports this argument and has concluded that there are cultural impacts as a result of the use of capital punishment within a nation (Bohm, 2017; Mfonobong, Bassey, & Okpe, 2019; Sarat, 2001; Steiker & Steiker, 2017). There tends to be national consensus on whether or not capital punishment should be employed (Steiker & Steiker, 2017). But support, or lack thereof, tends to originate from structural sources (Cao, Lai, & Huang, 2020). Attitudes and beliefs are reflected within the composition of a nation, including the use of capital punishment on criminal offenders. And these attitudes and beliefs are part of the moral norms of the nation (Mfonobong, Bassey, & Okpe, 2019). Members of a nation may turn to political leaders for direction in the nature of how to treat other members of the nation.

Political leaders establish the laws of the nation (Cao, Lai, & Huang, 2020; Mfonobong, Bassey, & Okpe, 2019). If these leaders emulate violence through the laws they establish as an accepted manner in which to treat criminal offenders, these leaders are exhibiting a justifiable use of violence to control member's behaviors. If violence is acceptable for controlling criminal behavior, why then wouldn't violence also be acceptable to control youth behavior? Prisoners are one of the most vulnerable members of a nation. Prisoners have restricted freedoms, if any at all. In many instances, incarceration is the equivalent of living in a cage with limited access to the world outside that cage. The norm is established that violence is acceptable to resolve conflict, particularly on the vulnerable members of society. And children are another vulnerable population within society.

Physical Discipline Most instances of child maltreatment are not officially reported (Widom, 1989). Therefore, combined with variance in definitions, there are severe limitations in trying to compare child maltreatment transnationally. Instead, the norms for a nation may be reflected within laws addressing child maltreatment. One law that can be viewed universally is whether or not the nation, as a whole, has laws addressing the use of corporal discipline against children.

The acts of physical discipline do not occur equally across different nations. There is some variation nation to nation, including the use of harsh physical discipline, i.e., hitting youth over and over again with a closed fist (Runyan et al., 2010). This is the equivalent of a criminal act in some nations when the person/entity being hit is not a child. A community member behaving deviously or violating the law would most likely not be hit by their neighbor as a method of social control. Undesirable behavior would be sanctioned with other, non-violent methods (e.g., verbally request the deviant behavior to stop, call authorities to intervene). What makes physical punishment against children acceptable?

The same arguments about capital punishment can be applied to physical punishment. Structural forces such as the law have an influence over the norms in a nation. If the laws supporting violence surround methods of social control, it stands to reason that other domains of society will follow suit. This includes socialization processes. Rather than physical punishment being deviant and viewed as harmful toward the development of children, the general membership of society may view physical discipline as necessary to control youth behavior. As discussed throughout this book, physical punishment of children is one dimension of violent socialization processes.

These examples of the cultural structure of a nation are forces creating a context in which violence is more of a norm in some nations. This contextual effect refers to conditions of violence within nations that shape methods of social control used by aggregates of families and communities within those nations. The conditions in a nation are unique, including social contexts (Petersen, Joseph, & Feit, 2014). And contexts have been shown to have a strong influence on youth criminal behavior (Fine, Mahler, Stein, Frick, & Cauffman, 2017). As outlined previously, there are a variety of factors that contribute to the context in which normative standards exist within a nation. The question is: What can be attributed to variation in youth criminal behaviors across different nations? This book argues violent socialization. This assertion must be tested to demonstrate its validity: *criminal behavior will significantly vary nation to nation as a function of violent socialization processes, serving within a context of norms of violence* (H_3).

Laws associated with violence or the prevention of violence are, alone, not sufficient indicators of norms of violence. Rather, norms of violence occur within a context and require multiple different indicators within any nation to reflect the norms. The conditions discussed here are not all encompassing of the perceived violence occurring within specific nations. Cultural differences make it difficult to measure and compare violence across nations (Eller, 2006). Other indicators of violence may include war/military action, mass media, and pop culture. For example, war has been argued to be a justifiable form of violence that contributes to higher instances of the use of illegitimate violence (Alvarez & Bachman, 2017). However, war is not a consistent measure transnationally. Nations do not necessarily experience war at the same time, nor is all military action defined as war. There are issues when trying to compare war within nations, particularly when the historical time and space that occupies conditions of war vary transnationally. This makes universal measures of violence necessary for transnational studies—to avoid issues with reliability and validity. Future studies can re-examine the theoretical proposition presented in this book from the lens of other indicators of violence, when those indicators become universal across nations and have standardized measures for violence.

Theoretically, violent socialization occurs within a context of any given nation and this contextual effect is part of the normative experiences within that nation. This context includes the criminal behavior that results from the victimization effect of violent socialization processes. The contextual effect is a norm of violence.

A New Theoretical Approach

Violence is an accepted part of culture (Heath, Kruttschnitt, & Ward, 1986). This can include the methods of social control within a nation. The newly proposed theory, norms of violence, takes an integrated social-control culture of violence perspective. The theory contends that socialization processes used as social control within pro-violent cultures are ineffective. Youth surrounded by a national context of social forces that legitimize violence to such a degree that the normative standards for socializing youth are embedded in violence, will engage in increased criminal behavior. This involves a combination of macro- to micro-level norms.

Contextual Effect of Living within a Specific Nation

The conditions specific to any nation create a context of acceptable boundaries for socialization processes, such as the extent to which violence is used within socialization processes. The location of a family, including the nation in which they reside, can influence socialization processes (Furstenburg, 1993). The community creates a context which influences the ability of individual families to function either effectively or ineffectively (Rutter, 1981). Violent methods of social control are part of a greater context in which violence, in general, is part of the conditions of a nation rather than confined to individual families. For example, violence against youth within individual families is influenced by the behaviors that occur within other individual families (Mackie & LeJeune, 2009). But when groups of families *all* disapprove violence against youth, an individual family tends to be less likely to engage in violence against youth due to communal disapproval (Mackie & LeJeune, 2009). This aggregate effect is but one condition contributing to the normalizing effect on violence.

Over time, violence becomes legitimized as sanctions for undesirable or deviant behavior, as well as an appropriate tactic for conflict resolution. This is another condition contributing to the normalizing effect on violence within a nation. This norm is reflected through the laws of a nation. As discussed earlier, the treatment of vulnerable members of society, as enacted in laws, reflects the level of civility in a nation. If laws are considered functional violence, the nation operates in a context that expects violence, needs violence, and argues for the use of violence. Violence is simply normal. The current approach of most criminological theories is that violence is dysfunctional. This is simply not the case.

National perspectives on violence vary. The contexts in which violence occur as justified and legitimized are variant transnationally. For example, violent socialization processes may be the "norm" within one nation, but considered deviant in another nation. Despite the use of physical discipline being considered violent behavior (Straus & Donnelly, 1994), the use of physical discipline to correct youth's behavior is still considered a norm within the United States (Zolotor, Theodore, Runyan, Chang, & Laskey, 2011) yet has been legally prohibited in Sweden (Gumbrecht, 2011). In fact, youth exposed to violence within the family have been considered victims of crime under Swedish law (Eriksson, 2010). This is a context specific to one dimension of violent socialization processes. But the argument can be extended to all the dimensions.

Methods of socializing youth are part of a broader social context, a context subject to the influence of the formal and informal structure of a nation. A national context effect is another condition reflective of normative standards within a nation. This involves community behaviors and structural standards. Some may argue that violence is nothing more than a shift in national perspectives. But change in society is slow. And these shifts are virtually nonexistent. There are very few countries that recognize violence as violence (Eller, 2006). Violence is entrenched within societies to such a degree that the normative standards for conflict resolution have some degree of violent reactions. The citizenry is not even aware that their way of life is embedded with violence. Such arguments of shifting definitions of violence fail to acknowledge the extent to which violence is normalized within, yet unrecognized by, society.

This is not a subcultural approach. Evolutionary psychologists claim aggressiveness is universal among primates (Aronson, 2012). Human beings are classified as primates. Violence, then, is part of human aggression. By extension, the argument can be made that violence is part of the human condition. This means that violence is normal, not deviant. Violence is not confined to a fraction of the members of a nation. Violence may simply be an acceptable way of life in some nations. And, as discussed previously, violence manifests in a variety of domains within nations.

The Spillover Effect

Different nations embrace different norms surrounding the acceptability of violence. This is not a new argument, per se. Straus (2001, 2004b) has argued elsewhere that when physical discipline is frequently used on youth, other forms of violence tend to be more acceptable. This is a context in which one form of violence may reproduce other forms of violence, including criminal behavior.

Straus has referred to this context of violence as both the criminogenic effect (2010) and the spillover effect (*cf.* Baron, Straus, & Jaffee, 1988).

This applies to the norms of violence thesis in that violence occurring within the methods of individual familial socialization processes may be associated with violent socialization occurring at the societal level (see Lansford & Dodge [2008]). The acceptance of violence as a method of social control at the macro level spills over into other domains of society. This includes communities and families. This spillover of structurally supported violence extends to socialization processes. Family sanctions are merely the result of society legitimizing violence. Under this assertion, violent socialization processes not only inculcate normative violence as social control, but reinforce and reproduce a culture of normative violence. Such conditions of violence render socialization ineffective at controlling youth behavior.

There has been research to support this spillover effect. For example, certain nation-based characteristics, such as widespread violence in the community, tend to influence the use of violence in resolving sexual conflict with an unwilling sexual partner (Lyndon, White, Kadlec, & Kelly, 2007). Another example is that youth chronically exposed to violence are more likely to engage in violent behavior compared to youth not exposed to violence (Spano, Rivera, & Bolland, 2010). But these particular findings may be limited in explaining the relationship between violent socialization and youth criminal behavior. Many studies restrict samples to singular nations. Yet the findings are consistent: youth exposure to a variety of dimensions of violence across multiple sources may be socialized into pro-violent orientations. These orientations may be consistent across the same nation while varying nation to nation.

As argued by Matsueda (2013), the macro-to-micro effect has not yet theoretically been fully developed. This may be because criminological research has not fully explored macro-to-micro explanations of crime, criminal behavior, and crime rates. This research is necessary in criminology. As stated previously in this book, characteristics that occur at a higher level (i.e., structural factors) can influence individual level characteristics (Luke, 2004). Further, interdependent relationships between multiple social factors best explain the degree to which youth are involved in criminal behavior (Baker, 2010). These factors include macro-to-micro attributes and outcomes. For the current study, aggregates of families engaging in similar socialization processes to control youth behavior may hold interdependency with the communities they reside. Aggregates of families engaging in ineffective familial socialization processes may simply be groups of vulnerable families residing within the same community (Bronfenbrenner, 1986). Further, the structure of the nation in which these communities are nested and aggregations of families reside may influence the nature of the socialization processes. Matsueda (2013) argues that cross-national criminology needs to look at the effect of macro-level factors on micro-level outcomes, while holding constant micro-level processes. This book fills these gaps in the current literature.

Straus' spillover theory focuses almost exclusively on the use of force in reference to violence. The focus seems to be implicit violence, with little consideration for latent manifestation of covert violence. Even when families are aggregated to represent groups clustered within nations, these aggregations do not fully represent the structure of a nation. There are other indicators of violence within the structure of nation, beyond individuals. The organization of the nation needs to be considered. As discussed previously, the structure within a nation also shapes socialization processes. This includes laws sanctioning violence as social control.

Much of the current literature, including studies specifically testing the spillover effect, contend that violence is deviant, illegitimate, or subcultural (see e.g., Baron & Straus, 1987; Baron, & Straus, 1988; Feld & Straus, 1989; Lysova & Straus, 2019; Straus, 1991; Straus, 2010; Straus, Douglas, & Medeiros, 2014; Straus, Gelles, & Steinmetz, 1980). The newly proposed theory takes the opposite position: violence is a norm. The norms of violence thesis expands on Straus' spillover effect. As he has argued since his first publications on the spillover effect, there is more theoretical explanation needed for violence (personal communication, December 6, 2015).

The Norms of Violence Thesis

The newly proposed theory is an integrated explanation of social control and culture of violence examining the influence of norms at both the macro- and micro-levels on social control. The main premise of the theory is that violence is more common within some nations and is, in fact, part of the norms of any given nation. The theory takes a functional approach in that violence serves a need within society. Families need to inculcate children into the norms of society as a preventative method for criminal behavior. Conceptually, proper socialization provides the external control necessarily to ward off youth criminal behavior while instilling a sense of internal control. This external control is influenced by the context in which the socialization occurs. Conditions within a nation that legitimize violence portray violence as a normalized standard, both at the macro-level (social structure) and the micro-level (e.g., family). When youth internalize the norms of society and these norms tolerate violence, youth may become traumatized (victimization from violence). The traumatic effect displays over time as acting out behaviors, including criminal behavior. The degree to which youth act out with criminal behavior varies based on the extent to which youth were exposed to violent socialization processes.

This exposure includes a national context of structural violence. Nations that support methods of violent social control or violent means for resolving conflict develop a normative standard favoring violent socialization processes and the members of that nation embrace this violence as a norm. Violent socialization processes then become part of the structural standards unique to a specific nation and families conform to such societal standards when socializing youth. As Durkheim noted, "society surpasses us, it obliges us to surpass ourselves" (1977[1914], p. 163). In other words, violent socialization processes may be the reproduction of social forces beyond individual families, and therefore behavior within individual families may be influenced by norms unique to a nation. Violent socialization intended to control and prevent youth criminal behavior is not a subculture, but rather part of the mainstream culture of a nation.

Current research indicates that structural factors do influence different types of criminal behavior (DeGue, DiLillo, & Scalora, 2010). There is also research indicating that there are structural patterns across nations in family violence (Eriksson, 2010), which includes some aspects of violent socialization processes. Theoretically, there is a macro-to-micro connection that contribute to youth criminal behavior. However, there seems to be a lack of research that specifically explores the effects of violent socialization processes on youth criminal behavior across different nations. The research present in this book will support the Norms of Violence thesis.

This theory also integrates ecological models. Under Bronfenbrenner's (1986) bio-ecological systems model, socialization processes do not operate independently. Neither families nor communities socialize youth in isolation. It is the combined efforts of the family, at a micro-level, and the community, at a macro-level, that operate within the context of the norms of the nation to prepare youth to be functioning members of society. And societal norms shape the socialization of youth independent of familial and communal socialization processes. For example, the social change currently occurring in some Asian and Pacific nations impacts the ability of that nation to exert control over youth behavior, including criminal behavior (Shaw, 2010). Just as the context of social change within a nation may be associated with an inability to control youth criminal behavior, the members of a nation responsible for socialization may be less able to adequately control youth behavior due to a context of societal norms of violence.

There is research that provides examples of socialization occurring within a context of societal norms, and specifically supports the norms of violence thesis. One area of socialization specific to norms of violence is the degree to which individuals tolerate violence within any given nation. Individual acceptance of violence against children tends to be influenced by national views that tolerate violence against children (e.g., see Gabarino, 1997; Lansford et al., 2005; Tang, 2006; Whipple & Richey, 1997). For example, across 32 nations, aggregates of mothers who claim to disapprove the use of physical discipline on children still consistently engaged in some form of physical discipline on their children to correct their children's behaviors (Cappa & Kahn, 2011). In some of these nations, the discipline used was so severe that it could be considered physical abuse (e.g., hitting the child with an object). The combination of international studies on physical discipline presented in this book found variation in the use of physical discipline across different nations.

These studies attribute this variation to nation-specific contexts. One specific context in which physical discipline occurred was the socioeconomic status of the *nation*, with families living in low- and middle-income nations engaging in more harsh corporal discipline than families living in high-income nations (see Cappa & Kahn, 2011; Runyan, et al., 2010). The studies describe a contextual effect for the use of physical discipline within the nation as a whole: socioeconomic conditions of nations influencing group-level methods of social control used within that nation. International research is beginning to show contextual effects in socialization processes specific to each individual nation. There are several other published international studies that specifically examine physical discipline/abuse across different nations (e.g., Gagné, Tourigny, Joly, & Pouliot-Lapointe, 2007; Jackson, et al., 1999; Qasem, Mustafa, Kazem, & Shah, 1998; Roberts, 2000). The results seem to reflect a pattern of variation nation to nation in the use of physical discipline, including extreme forms (i.e., physical abuse). This indicates a possible national-context effect. Ultimately, violent familial socialization processes may occur within a context where the tendency toward violent behavior may be nation specific, and one aspect of norms for aggregates of families within that nation.

Despite the aforementioned studies finding variation in socialization processes, and specifically the use of physical discipline, across different nations, none of these studies specifically analyzed data to determine if there was significant variation nation to nation. Most of these studies used descriptive statistics to compare differences in the use of physical discipline by nation. These analyses, in essence, look only at differences in individual behavior within each nation rather than examine the context that compares differences among aggregates of families and communities nation to nation in combination with structural influences for that nation. In order to examine similarities and differences across different nations, analyses must include tests for interdependence (Bicchieri & Chavez, 2010).

The norms of violence thesis provide for a context of structural indicators of pro-violence conditions within a nation (macro-level) that spill-over into the socialization of youth contributing to violent social processes used within communities and aggregates of families (micro-level) to control youth behavior. The unintended consequence of this cross-level normative standards of violence is a victimizing effect that fails to prevent youth criminal behavior. In addition to Straus' comments about the need for more theoretical research on violence, Gottfredson discusses the need to "constantly question" theories of crime, including self-control theory, in order to remain consistent with current literature (2005, p. 78). There is published research supporting some of the basic contentions of the norms of violence thesis, for both youth and adult criminal behavior (e.g., see Delaney, 2015; Delaney, 2021a; Delaney, 2021b). This book offers the full theoretical proposition and provides the research needed to test the possibility that transnational variation of violence occurs within socialization processes, and the extent to which these violent socialization processes prevent or predict youth criminal behavior.

Violent Socialization as Part of a Norm of Violence

Violent socialization processes as the method used to control youth behavior is one aspect of the "norms of violence" thesis. Much of violence is a way of life within some nations. Violence may be instrumental within some nations: a means to an end. Violent socialization processes, violence is instrumental. The intended goals of violent socialization processes are not necessary to cause pain or harm, but rather to control youth behavior. The manner in which youth are socialized, both directly and indirectly, can demonstrate the extent to which the covert manifestations of violence permeate from the culture and structure of a nation in an obscured manner. This makes looking at violence as a force alone insufficient. In combination with the failure to examine the macro-to-micro connection, theories trying to explain the link between cultural violence and youth criminal behavior fail to consider contribution of the victimizing effect of violence within society.

There is literature spanning decades that explores cross-national socialization (e.g., Douglas & Straus, 2006; Montague, 1978); the current literature does not appear to have examined specifically whether or not youth criminal behavior varies when violent socialization processes are part of norms transnationally. Violent familial socialization processes could vary across different nations, and, therefore, the effects of violent familial socialization processes could be associated with variation in criminal behavior. The current literature shows that familial socialization processes, in general, *do* vary across different nations (e.g., Keller, Otto, Lamm, Yovsi, & Kartner, 2008; Urquiza & Goodlin-Jones, 1994) and this variation in familial socialization processes has been associated with influencing the degree to which youth may engage in criminal behavior (Maughan & Gardner, 2010). Socialization processes amalgamate with other conditions within a nation. Violence may be deep-rooted within these conditions producing increased criminal behavior among youth.

Norms or Social Learning?

A reasonable argument could be made that violent socialization processes may actually be associated with social learning theories. For example, many experts in the field of family violence support the idea that "violence begets violence" (Widom, 1989). Adults using violence may inadvertently be teaching youth that violence is an acceptable method to resolve conflict (*cf.* Straus & Donnelly, 1994). Social learning theory is a micro-level theory to explain why youth engage in criminal behavior. The norms of violence thesis argues, instead, a macro-to-micro-level integrated social control-culture of violence theory in which motivation is not a factor contributing to youth criminal behavior. The social control aspect recognizes that it is human nature to engage in deviance, violence, and criminal acts. Youth need to be socialized to control their behavior, delay gratification, and inculcate a level of self-control. The culture of violence aspect recognizes that some nations have more pro-violent structures within their organization. These societies have integrated violence as a means to resolve conflict, address deviance, and control youth behavior. Learning theories argue that you must actively learn all aspects of being a member of a nation, including violence. Norms of violence theory simply argue that violence is the lifestyle of the nation spilling over into the institutions that comprise the nation's structure and act to control youth behavior.

The norms of violence thesis also do not consider the relationships youth form later in life, such as with peers. The theory is not about association with peers (e.g., differential association theory) nor about reinforcing the learning of criminal behavior through rewards and punishment (e.g., differential association reinforced). The theory does not take a stance on punishment as deterrence to prevent youth criminal behavior (e.g., see Akers, 1990). Socialization is not about modeling behaviors, but rather about social control. Norms of violence is not learned. It is the standard across a nation for a variety of violence-based conditions, supported within communities and families, that fail to prevent youth criminal behavior. Violence is normalized and present, not specifically learned. Transmission of the conditions of a nation may be present, but these transmissions are subtle inculcations rather than active lessons. Violent socialization processes are not the equivalent of teaching youth deviant behaviors or youth learning violent behavior. Violent familial socialization processes are the absence of effective socialization.

Consequences for Norms of Violence

The norms of violence theses take a dual approach: victimization and criminal behavior of youth. Children exposed to violence victimize the youth by translating into normative behavioral responses (Gorman-Smith & Tolan, 1998) such as criminal behavior. The effect is not limited to the family during primary socialization, but rather is the cumulative impact of the totality of pro-violent conditions within a nation that spill-over into familial socialization processes. This spillover influences behavioral responses toward conflict, and the victimizing effect exasperates violent responses to conflict (Delaney, 2021b). There is literature that explores cross-national socialization and criminal behavior (e.g., Douglas & Straus, 2006; Montague, 1978); the current literature does not appear to have examined specifically whether or not youth criminal behavior varies when violent socialization processes are part of norms of violence cross-nationally.

The main argument of the book is to examine the context in which violence is the norm within a nation. This book does not measure cultural conceptions of violence individual to each nation. A secondary argument in this book is that the pro-violent conditions within a nation produce a victimizing effect of normalized violence for youth. These dual forces may be so potent that nations with a higher presence of normalized violence may contribute to youth who tend to be involved in more criminal behavior compared to youth from nations in which violence does not penetrate multiple spheres of society. Such conditions within any given nation may communally transfer norms across all boundaries. Research is needed to examine these hypothesized relationships. The remaining chapters in this book present the research needed to examine the extent to which cross-national variation within socialization processes, including violence, is associated with preventing or predicting criminal behavior among youth.

It is the work of criminologists to test theories to determine the validity of conceptualized measures. The explicit claims of this newly proposed theory need to be tested to determine the veracity of such claims across different nations. None of the studies presented from the current literature, nor the present study, seek to answer the issue of causal order when explaining crime and criminal behavior. If the causes of criminal behavior were known, there would be no further need to examine theories of criminal behavior. A definitive solution for risk factors would prevail and prevent youth criminal behavior. Instead, the current study explores the relationship between violent socialization processes and youth criminal behavior to offer a new theory that explains the victimization-criminal behavior connection transnationally. Criminology is still strongly influenced by theoretical explanations and empirical studies designed to support or disprove these theories. As such, the present study contributes to the study of criminology by beginning a preliminary analysis of a context in norms of violence within any given nation that may be associated with variation in youth criminal behavior. This is one of the first studies to test an integrated social control-culture of violence theory. The analysis will be based on multiple dimensions of violence within socialization processes and the structural conditions of a nation.

Chapter 4

Methodology

The study of crime is still strongly influenced by theoretical explanations of criminal behavior and the empirical studies designed to support or disprove these theories. If the causes of criminal behavior were known, then there would be no further need to examine theories explaining criminal behavior, nor risk factors for criminal behavior and victimization. The present work contributes to the study of criminology by beginning a preliminary analysis of a context in which norms of violence within any given nation may be associated with variation in criminal behavior. This study does not seek to answer the issue of causal order. Socialization processes are ongoing and continue throughout the life course. With this consideration, socialization begins during childhood and childhood is a life course stage before adolescence. In the sense of temporal order, socialization occurs first, to some extent, before adolescent youth engage in criminal behavior. Thus, while the present study is an exploration into the association between violent socialization processes and criminal behavior among late adolescent youth, this study is expected to support the theory of norms of violence.

The following three hypotheses are being tested:

H_1: youth from families that use violent socialization processes will engage in more criminal behavior, compared to youth from families that do not use violent socialization processes even in the presence of effective social control markers;
H_2: youth in communities that use violent socialization processes will engage in more criminal behavior, compared to youth in communities that do not use violent socialization processes; and
H_3: criminal behavior will significantly vary nation to nation as a function of violent socialization processes, serving within a context of norms of violence.

To test these hypotheses, a secondary data analysis is being used on the archived data from the International Dating Violence Study (Straus & Members of the International Dating Violence Research Consortium, 2004). The International

Dating Violence Study has a rich compilation of variables measuring violence, social control, familial socialization, and criminal behavior that is not available from any other readily accessible international datasets.

Dataset

The International Dating Violence Study (IDVS) dataset is a cross-sectional, international convenience sample of over 17,000 college and university students in 32 different nations. Table 4.1 lists each of the nations included in the dataset, and the number and percentage of respondents within each of these nations. Conducted between 2001 and 2006, this dataset contains anonymous demographic and descriptive self-reported information about students enrolled in a variety of classes in various social science departments (e.g., criminology,

Table 4.1 Number and Percent of Respondents from Each Nation (IDVS)

Country	*Abbreviation code*	*N*	*% of respondents*
Australia	(AST)	210	0.3
Belgium	(BEL)	574	0.7
Brazil	(BRZ)	275	0.8
Canada	(CND)	1199	0.7
China	(CHN)	2502	1.0
England	(ENG)	218	1.4
Germany	(GER)	471	3.5
Greece	(GRC)	286	1.8
Guatemala	(GTL)	249	1.6
Hungary	(HUN)	176	1.1
India	(IND)	190	1.2
Iran	(IRN)	99	0.6
Israel	(ISR)	153	1.0
Japan	(JPN)	207	1.3
Lithuania	(LTH)	448	2.9
Malta	(MLT)	112	0.7
Mexico	(MEX)	235	0.7
The Netherlands	(NTL)	410	1.5
New Zealand	(NZL)	137	0.9
Portugal	(PGL)	424	2.7
Romania	(ROM)	271	1.7
Russia	(RSS)	450	2.9
Scotland	(SCT)	213	1.4
Singapore	(SNG)	231	1.5
S. Africa	(SAF)	124	0.8
S. Korea	(SKR)	243	1.6
Sweden	(SWD)	433	2.8
Switzerland	(SWZ)	161	3.4
Taiwan	(TWN)	258	1.6
Tanzania	(TAN)	208	1.3
United States	(USA)	4236	27.1
Venezuela	(VNZ)	249	1.6

family studies, psychology, sociology) from different colleges and universities around the world. These post-secondary institutions were locations where members of the International Dating Violence Research Consortium were employed. More information about the details of the International Dating Violence Study can be located at https://doi.org/10.3886/ICPSR29583.v1.

Sample

Although the original dataset contains 17,404 cases, some of the respondents were older than the age-frame consistent with late adolescence. Cases outside the age range from 17 years to 25 years were removed to help limit memory bias. The dataset also contained cases with missing data, due to non-response on certain survey items. Since deleting cases tends to produce the least biased parameter estimates and standard errors compared to imputation (Allison, 2002), these cases were also removed from the dataset. Finally, in the construction of the self-control scale (see variables section below), there were an additional 3,012 cases that were removed. After filtering the data and removing all these cases, the final sample size became 12,640 respondents in 32 nations.

Some criminologists have argued that using samples of college and university students to study crime does not produce valid results (e.g., see Hagan & McCarthy, 1997; Payne & Chappell, 2009). However, other criminologists argue that self-reported criminal behavior among samples of college students tends to be similar to the self-reported criminal behavior among comparable youth not in college. For example, to examine the validity of this comparable result argument, Wiecko (2010) compared responses for college students and non-college students between ages 17 and 25 years on several different items measuring criminal behavior. He found almost no statistically significant differences in self-reported criminal behavior between the groups, and only minor differences in frequency of criminal behavior between college students and youth of the same age frame not in college. Wiecko (2010) concluded that samples of college students, while perhaps unique in extending and maintaining their adolescence (Moffatt, 1991) as well as other aspects of social identity (Payne & Chappell, 2009) compared to other youth populations, do not produce invalid results in the study of crime. Specific to the IDVS data, Straus (2004a; 2009) found that samples not nationally representative of the general population can still provide valid results. Using the theoretical concept of a national context effect, Straus analyzed the validity of the IDVS data by comparing the correlation between the results of the IDVS measures to independent measures from different international samples. He tested concurrent validity, using national-level data and measures associated with violence and crime, and construct validity, to compare the results from 41 studies to the IDVS data. Straus (2009) found all the IDVS measures to have concurrent validity. Further, the IDVS measures were consistent with the results from each of the 41 comparative studies, which supported construct validity. Despite the

IDVS data being a convenience sample of college students across 32 different nations, valid empirical conclusions can be drawn about international variation in criminal behavior using data from the IDVS. So, although the use of convenience samples tends to be a limitation, the present study may still present valid information about the extent to which violent socialization processes predict criminal behavior, and if criminal behavior varies as a function of norms of violence internationally, at least for this sample of youth.

Theoretical Concepts of the IDVS

The IDVS was intended to measure the prevalence and chronicity of dating violence and the risk factors associated with dating partner violence internationally (Straus & Members of the International Dating Violence Research Consortium, 2004). This includes information related to a range of behaviors, and variables measuring respondents' attitudes and values. The IDVS also includes measures to test several different criminological theories, one of which is Gottfredson and Hirschi's self-control theory (M. Straus, personal communication, January 22, 2010).

Other international datasets, including representative samples, fail to measure the full array of variables necessary to explore the relationship between violent socialization process and criminal behavior, as well as the theoretical framework of social control theories. For example, data from the International Social Survey Program (i.e., International Social Science Survey) provides family-based information in the most recent "Family and Changing Gender Roles III (International Social Survey Programme, (2019))" dataset. But the data do not include information about respondents' familial socialization processes or experiences with violent socialization. Rather, the data focus on topics related to employment, motherhood, and responsibility for child-rearing; alternative family forms; and division of household labor and decision-making surrounding child-rearing (see https://www.gesis.org/issp/modules/issp-modules-by-topic/family-and-changing-gender-roles/2012 for more information). Therefore, the IDVS provides the most accessible data set for capturing various different variables representing key components of violent socialization processes under the conceptual framework for the proposed *norms of violence* theory.

Variables

Most variables originate from the original dataset of the IDVS. These variables are derived from the Personal Relationship Profile scales (PRP), included within the IDVS. Table 4.2 lists each scale used and the individual items comprising each of the scales. These scales are pre-constructed within the dataset. As recommended by many researchers (see Ember & Ember, 1994), these scales offer standardized measures of violence and crime.

Table 4.2 Items from the Personal Relationships Profile (PRP) Scales

Concept	*PRP scale*
Youth Criminal Behavior	criminal history, Early onset sub-scale
Before age 15, I stole or tried to steal something worth more than $50.00	
Before age 15, I stole money (from anyone, including family)	
Before age 15, I physically attacked someone with the idea of seriously hurting them	
Before age 15, I hit or threatened to hit my parents	
Violent Familial Socialization	violent socialization, family subscale
When I was less than 12 years old, I was spanked or hit a lot by my mother or father	
When I was a teenager, I was hit a lot by my mother or father	
When I was a kid, I saw an adult in my family push, shove, slap, or throw something at someone	
When I was a kid, I saw my mother or father kick, punch, or beat up their partner	
My father or mother told me to hit back if someone hit me or insulted me	
Self-Control	self-control
I don't think about how what I do will affect other people (R)	
I often do things that other people think are dangerous (R)	
I have trouble following the rules at work or in school (R)	
I often get hurt by things that I do (R)	
I have goals in life that I try to reach	
Attachment	positive parenting
My parents did not help me to do my best in school (R)	
My parents did not care if I got into trouble in school (R)	
My parents did not comfort me when I was upset (R)	
My parents helped me when I had problems	
Violent Community Socialization	violent socialization, non-family subscale
When I was a kid, I often saw kids who were not in my family get into fights and hit each other	
When I was a kid, people not part of my family pushed, shoved, or slapped me, or threw things at me	
When I was a kid, people not part of my family told me to hit back if someone hit me or insulted me.	
Social Desirability	limited disclosure scale
I sometimes try to get even rather than forgive and forget (R)	
There have been occasions when I took advantage of someone (R)	
There have been times when I was quite jealous of the good fortune of others (R)	
I sometimes feel resentful when I don't get my way (R)	
I am sometimes irritated by people who ask favors of me (R)	
There have been times when I have felt like rebelling against people in authority even though I knew they were right (R)	
I have never deliberately said something that hurt someone's feelings	
No matter who I am talking to I am always a good listener	
On a few occasions, I have given up doing something because I thought too little of my ability(R)	
I have never been irked when people expressed ideas very different from my own	
It is sometimes hard for me to go on with my work if I am not encouraged (R)	
I am always courteous, even to people who are disagreeable	
I'm always willing to admit it when I make a mistake	

(R) indicates the item was reverse coded.

Given that the present study examines socialization through an international perspective, there is the possibility that these variables may be interpreted differently across the nations. To mitigate for this possibility, each survey item was translated from a member of the Consortium at the institution in which the survey was administered then back-translated to ensure conceptual equivalence (Gàmez-Guadix, Straus, & Hershberger, 2011) across each nation.

Measures

The present study uses the PRP scales to increase precision in measuring various dimensions (Singleton & Straits, 1988) of violent familial socialization processes. The goal is to minimize measurement error by limiting mono-operation bias (Shadish, Cook, & Campbell, 2002) among these complex variables. Table 4.3 lists the descriptive statistics for all the variables used in this study. There are limitations of conducting analyses on archived data, such as the inability to manage the performance of the measures. The measures for each of the predictor and dependent variables are created by someone else (Shadish, Cook, & Campbell, 2002), and could be subject to bias. Each scale was tested previously and demonstrated reliability and validity cross-culturally (see Straus [2004a] for details).

Table 4.3 Descriptive Statistics

	Minimum	*Maximum*	*Mean*	*Standard Deviation*
OLS and MLM level-1 (n = 12,640)				
violent comm	8.00	32.00	14.61	4.01
violent family/vsfamily	5.00	20.00	8.38	2.68
attachments	4.00	16.00	13.43	2.22
self-control	9.00	24.00	19.47	2.61
gender	0	1.00	0.30	0.46
age	18.00	25.00	21.11	2.50
peer crime	0	1.00	0.54	0.50
SES	−3.20	3.60	0.036	0.98
social desire	13.00	44.00	28.36	3.93
Criminal Behavior scale	4.00	16.00	5.71	2.03
t-tests and MLM level-2 (n = 32)				
violent socialization	6.56	10.02	8.26	0.87
vscommunity	3.00	12.00	6.23	1.90
discipline	0	1.00	0.63	0.48
death penalty	0	1.00	0.41	0.49
homicide rate	0	49.56	5.43	7.92
GDP	1.00	5.00	3.62	1.60
Criminal Behavior scale	4.93	7.10	5.85	2.22

Youth Criminal Behavior

Youth criminal behavior, the dependent variable, was measured by self-reported answers to items inquiring about property crime and violent crime (i.e., assault) occurring before the respondent turned 15. The degree to which individuals engage in criminal behavior tends to vary over the life course (Laub & Sampson, 2003). The present study took such considerations into account, by limiting the time frame for offending behavior to strictly juveniles (minority status). This exclusion criterion helps to make the measure more consistent across nations, as the age of majority varies from nation to nation (Unicef, 2016). Example items include "I stole or tried to steal something worth more than $50.00"[1] and "I physically attacked someone with the idea of seriously hurting them." Using the early onset subscale of the criminal history scale, scores for these items are based on the respondent's level of agreement that they had engaged in property crime or violent crime before age 15, ranging from strongly disagree (1) to strongly agree (4). Due to high positive skew, this scale was transformed by the natural log. This produced a more normal distribution.

Violent Socialization Processes

The measures of violent socialization processes involve three separate variables: violent familial socialization, violent socialization in the community, and total violent socialization during childhood. Each of these variables are from the violent socialization scales of the personal and relationships profile (see Straus, Hamby, Boney-McCoy, & Sugarman, 2010), included in the International Dating Violence Study dataset. Each variable was measured on a 4-point Likert scale, with response categories ranging from strongly disagree to strongly agree. Higher scores indicate more experiences of violent socialization. Differences in each of these variables are explained below, as well as alterations made to each variable for the different analyses.

VIOLENT SOCIALIZATION WITHIN THE FAMILY

This main predictor variable is measured using the family subscale for the violent socialization scale. This subscale has five items, measuring the degree to which the individual respondents agree that they experienced direct or vicarious victimization within the family, as well as being counseled by the family to engage in violence to resolve conflict. These items include being hit frequently by parents both prior to age 12 (1) and as a teenager (2), witnessing violence by both a parent (3) and other non-parent family member (4), and being advised by a parent to use violence to resolve conflict (either violent or verbal) (5). These parental "acts" are better measures associated with criminal behavior than youth's attitudes or youth's prior behavior (Morris, Gerber, & Menard, 2011). This *vsfamily* scale represents respondents' experience with violent socialization processes within their individual families. Other studies testing social control theories, as related to familial socialization processes, have used similar measures, including excessive corporal discipline (Teague, Mazerolle, Legosz, & Sanderson, 2008) and parental physical abuse (Rebellon & Van Gundy, 2005).

This variable is used in two analyses: multilevel modeling (MLM) and ordinary least squares regression (OLS). For MLM, this variable is a level-1 predictor (*vsfamily*). Since the intercept from the level-1 analysis becomes an outcome in the level-2 analysis of multilevel modeling regression analysis (Luke, 2004), *vsfamily* is centered on the grand-mean of all individual cases in order to provide meaningful interpretation of true values for the dependent variable (Jones & Subramanian, 2019; Singer & Willett, 2003). For OLS regression analysis (*violent family*), the variable is left unaltered.

Violent Socialization within the Community. This second main predictor variable is measured using the community subscale for the violent socialization scale. This subscale contains three items: experiencing violence from non-family; witnessing peer violence; and members being advised by non-family members to use violence to resolve conflict, either violent or verbal. The variable measures youth responses about experiences with violent socialization within their community, both direct and vicarious experiences. This is a proxy measure for violent socialization occurring within each nation. While this proxy is not representative of all members of a nation overall, this indicator is being used to explore the presence of variation in violent community socialization processes used within and between different nations.

This variable is used in two analyses: multilevel modeling (MLM) and ordinary least squares regression (OLS). For MLM, this variable is a level-2 predictor (*vscommunity*). Responses are aggregated nationally by averaging the responses for all respondents within each nation. The result is a group-level mean of violent community socialization processes for each of the 32 nations. *Vscommunity* is then centered on the grand mean of all nations, so that scores range from less violent community socialization (−3.38) to more violent community socialization (11.62) with an average of zero (0). This centering was necessary in order to provide meaningful interpretation of true values for the dependent variable (Singer & Willett, 2003). This predictor variable is also used in ordinary least squares regression analysis, but in the original scale form (i.e., not aggregated or centered).

Violent socialization. To fully test the "norms of violence" thesis, comparisons need to be made between violent socialization processes and other indicators of violence. A third variable, *violent socialization*, represents all violent socialization processes for each respondent within each of the nations. *Violent socialization* is a scale that combines both violent socialization within the family and in the community. This dependent variable has been altered to become the aggregated response for all respondents within each nation, i.e., the group-level mean of all violent socialization processes within each of the 32 nations. Violent socialization is an outcome variable for different bivariate statistical tests. This variable is not used in the regression analysis, in order to prevent multicollinearity.

Legal Status of Physical Discipline

This indicator measures whether or not each nation has laws prohibiting the use of physical discipline on children. This aggregate measure (*discipline*) was used to explore one aspect of violence occurring within nations: legal support for the use of violence against others. As outlined in the previous chapter, the physical discipline of children is considered violence in some nations, while considered a norm in other nations. Not all nations prohibit the use of physical discipline on children. Among those nations that have laws prohibiting physical discipline, these laws vary in implementation from nation to nation: some nations prohibit the use of physical discipline within schools, while other nations prohibit the use of physical discipline both within schools and by families.

To obtain information about the legal status of physical discipline on children, data were derived from the Global Initiative to End All Corporal Punishment of Children (2012) organization's website. This website lists the legal status of corporal discipline across 172 nations, including all nations contained in the IDVS dataset. This variable was coded such that nations that have any laws prohibiting any physical discipline on children were coded 1, and nations without these laws were coded 0. It should be noted that some of these nations passed anti-physical punishment laws prior to data collection for the IDVS. Other nations passed the laws during data collection (e.g., Hungary's law was enacted in 2004). Five nations passed anti-physical punishment laws after data had been collected for the IDVS. This does not mean that collective public sentiment toward the use of physical discipline on children was established in close relation to the date these laws were enacted. Rather, as discussed in the previous chapter, laws may take years to create due to changing norms within a nation. This indicator variable was used in bivariate statistical tests to assess the "norms of violence" thesis and as a control variable in regression analysis. See the "analysis" section.

Legal Status of the Death Penalty

This indicator measures whether or not each nation has laws prohibiting the use of the death penalty on those convicted of crimes. This aggregate measure (*death penalty*) was used to explore another separate aspect of violence occurring within nations: state-sanctioned and administrated violent punishment. Data were derived from both the Death Penalty Information Center (2012) and the Cornell Center on the Death Penalty Worldwide (2020). These websites list the legal status of corporal punishment across all recognized nations. All of the nations in the IDVS prohibiting the use of the death penalty enacted the legal ban prior to or during data collection for the IDVS. As stated previously, the laws of a nation may take years to create due to changing norms within a nation, and laws that were enacted during data collection may be national sentiments from previous years.

This variable was coded such that nations that have abolished the use of the death penalty were coded 1, and nations still having laws allowing for the use of the death penalty were coded 0. It should be noted that one of the 32 nations, South Korea, has not abolished laws permitting the use of the death penalty. While South Korea has not engaged in any state-sanctioned criminal execution since 1997 (The Cornell Center on the Death Penalty Worldwide, 2020) and would be considered a *de facto* abolitionist nation, use of the death penalty is still possible. Therefore, death penalty data for South Korea was coded as missing. This indicator variable was used in bivariate statistical tests to assess the "norms of violence" thesis and as a control variable in regression analysis. See the "analysis" section.

Homicide Rate

The rate of intentional homicide in each nation was used to explore a third unique aspect of violence occurring within nations: violent crime. Intentional homicide is defined, internationally, as the intended illegal killing of an individual by another individual (United Nations, 2012). Given that the laws defining crime vary from nation to nation, homicide data tends to be the most valid crime measure across different nations (LaFree, 2005). With a consistent definition of homicide across all nations, based on INTERPOL definitions (United Nations Office on Drugs and Crime, 2020), homicide rates are also a reliable measure.

Data were derived from the United Nations Office on Drugs and Crime's website (http://www.unodc.org/unodc/en/data-and-analysis/homicide.html). This website lists the rate of intentional homicides, per 100,000 in the population, for each of the 207 nations in the world between 1995 and 2011. To create the variable (*crime rate*), the intentional homicide rate for each nation was averaged over a period of 10 years (1996–2006) to produce a mean homicide rate for each nation. These years encompass five years prior to data collection for the IDVS and the five years in which data was collected for the IDVS. This variable was used in bivariate statistical tests to assess the "norms of violence" thesis, and as a control variable for regression analysis. See the "analysis" section.

Controls

Several other control variables typical for criminological research were included to rule out spurious relationships between the predictor variables and criminal behavior. As discussed in previous chapters, there can be an unlimited number of considerations when examining violence transnationally. One study cannot be expected to address all possible confounds (Shadish, Cook, & Campbell,

2002). Other cultural influences, such as politics and religion, if universally defined could be considered correlates of violence. The IDVS was not intended as a descriptive dataset; rather, the data was collected to test various theories of crime (Dawson & Straus, 2011).

Attachment

The second main predictor variable was measured using the positive parenting scale. This scale was designed to measure parental affection and support, by reverse coding some of the response categories for six items in the PRP neglect scale[2] in order to represent positive parenting practices rather than parental neglect (Straus, Hamby, Boney-McCoy, & Sugarman, 2010). Table 4.2 lists each item in this scale.

This positive parenting scale represents the degree to which respondents developed a bond with their family. The measure has been used in other studies to represent "good parenting" (Rebellon, Straus, & Medeiros, 2008). Previous studies have used similar measures to represent "attachment" within the family, including parental emotional support (Jensen, 1973), parental affection (Thompson & Dodder, 1983; Thompson & Dodder, 1986), relationship quality (Rebellon & Van Gundy, 2005), and parental praise (Beaver & Wright, 2007). This variable, unaltered, will be used in ordinary least squares regression analysis. For multilevel modeling regression analysis, described in "analysis" section later, *attachment* will be a level-1 variable that will function as an individual level predictor, and therefore was centered on the grand-mean of all individual cases for meaningful interpretation in multilevel modeling regression analysis.

Self-control

Self-control was measured using the self-control scale in the PRP. This scale includes six items measuring the elements of Gottfredson and Hirschi's General Theory of Crime (1990): self-centeredness, risk-taking, temper, physicality, impulsivity, ignoring; and long-term consequences. Some variables were reverse coded to retain measurement consistency across the scale. Items in the scale are listed in Table 4.2. This self-control scale was used in a previous study to specifically test Gottfredson and Hirschi's General Theory of Crime (Rebellon, Straus, and Medeiros, 2008).

One item, "there is nothing I can do to control my feelings when my partner hassles me," was not included in the "self-control" scale within the present study for three reasons. First, this item reflects anger in relation to an intimate partner only, and not all respondents were involved in an intimate relationship. Second, the item was asked only of the respondents who reported being in an intimate relationship rather than all respondents. This excludes 3,012 cases, and these cases were removed from the dataset. Exclusion criteria are sometimes necessary to ensure construct validity (Grimes & Schutz, 2005). In order to increase the likelihood that the construct "self-control" adequately reflects each individual respondent's ability to self-regulate their *own* behavior, the item was removed from the "self-control" scale. This exclusion criterion should assist with limiting the chances of construct validity threat and instead identify the correct construct (Shadish, Cook, & Campbell, 2002).

To determine the psychometric properties of this new scale, Factor Analysis was used with Varimax rotation and Kaiser normalization. The results, listed in Table 4.4, show the scale contains at least three or more significant factor loadings, indicating a single reliable latent dimension. Varimax converged high loadings for the four items on the first unrotated factor (Carmines & Zeller, 1979). Several other methods were used to test for reliability and validity of each of the scales, including Cronbach's alpha coefficient and inter-item correlations. The four items in the self-control scale were then combined into an additive scale with scores ranging from less individual self-control (5) to more individual self-control (20). The internal consistency reliability score for this scale was $\alpha = .624$. The inter-item correlations, shown in Table 4.5, show that each of the items in the self-control scale is significantly correlated, indicating these items are interrelated and valid measures (Hamilton, 1992) of individual self-control. Together, these three analyses demonstrate that the different items

Table 4.4 Rotated Components Loadings for Items in the *Self-Control* Scale (n = 12,640)

Ignoring	.729
Physicality	.687
Impulsivity	.650
Self-centeredness	.539
Long-term consequences	.410
Eigenvalue	1.886
% of total variance	37.714
α	.624

Table 4.5 Correlations Matrixes for Items in the *Self-Control* Scale (n = 12,640)

Self-control *scale*	*1*	2	3	4
do dangerous things (R)	–			
have trouble following rules (R)	.34**	–		
often hurt by things I do (R)	.30**	0.32**	–	
have goals in life I try to reach	.06**	0.19**	0.18**	–

** p≤0.01 * p≤0.05

(R) reverse coded

within each of the scales are related to each other (Schreiner & Louis, 2006) in measuring each individual dimension (Singleton & Straits, 1988) and thus warrant the creation of each scale.

Other studies testing self-control used similar measures of self-control (e.g., see Grasmick, Tittle, Bursik, & Arneklev, 1993). This main predictor variable, *self-control*, will be used, unaltered, in ordinary least squares regression analysis. As a level-1 predictor in multilevel modeling regression analysis, *self-control* was centered on the grand-mean of all individual cases. See the "analysis" section below.

Peer Involvement in Criminal Behavior

The importance of peer relationships may be particularly salient during adolescence. Some may argue that peers, particularly during late adolescence and emerging adulthood, provide more support and group cohesion than the family. Hence, to control for the effect of peer group influence on criminal behavior and rule out arguments that peers with criminal behavior might pose more influence over behaviors at this stage of the life course than the family (*cf.* differential association theory [Sutherland & Cressey, 1978]), this variable was measured as whether or not the respondent associates with peers who engage in criminal behavior. Two variables, "I have friends who committed crimes" and "I spend time with criminal friends," were dichotomized from four response categories (i.e., strongly disagree, disagree, agree, strongly agree) to two response categories (i.e., disagree or agree). This new variable represents respondents' agreement that their friends have criminal behavior or they associate with friends that engage in criminal behavior. This variable will be used in both ordinary least squares and multilevel modeling regression analyses.

Gender

Individual-level controls include the sex of the respondent. The original variable in the IDVS was re-coded to males (1) and females (0). This variable is used in both ordinary least squares and multilevel modeling regression analyses.

Age

Another individual-level control is the age of the respondent. This variable was included within the IDVS, but it was filtered to include the youth aged 17–25 (as described in the sample section above). This variable will be used in both ordinary least squares and multilevel modeling regression analyses. As a level-1 variable in multilevel modeling regression analysis, *age* was centered on the grand-mean of all individual cases in order to provide meaningful interpretation of true values for the dependent variable.

Socioeconomic Status

Socioeconomic status (*ses*), another control variable, consists of a scale combining both the father's and mother's completed education with the family's yearly income for each respondent. Scores range from low to high. This variable is used in both ordinary least squares and multilevel modeling regression analyses. As a level-1 variable in multilevel modeling regression analysis, *ses* was centered on the grand-mean of all individual cases in order to provide meaningful interpretation of true values for the dependent variable.

Social Desirability

Another control variable includes the limited disclosure scale to control for socially desirable responses. It is possible that some of the respondents may have answered questions in a manner that might make them look favorable rather than answering truthfully. Research has shown that questionnaires inquiring about both personal (Reynolds, 1982) and sensitive information (Lee, 1993) are subject to social desirability bias (Crowne & Marlowe, 1960). Therefore, the limited disclosure scale included items that measure for the possibility of respondents providing false answers about sensitive information for a more favorable personal image, such as underreporting criminal behavior.

This scale was based on an adaptation of Reynolds' short form of the Crowne-Marlow scale (Straus, Hamby, Boney-McCoy, & Sugarman, 2010). All 13 items from the limited disclosure scale were included for the social desirability scale. Higher scores represent more socially desirable responses. This variable is used in both ordinary least squares and multilevel modeling regression analyses. Because this is a continuous variable, the scale was centered on the grand-mean of all individual cases for the MLM regression analysis.

Gross Domestic Product

This variable, *GDP*, is an original IDVS variable. *GDP* was created using data from the United Nations Development Programme's Human development report of 1999, measuring the percent of national monies spent on the military compared to national monies spent on education and human services (Straus & Ramirez, 2000). The variable represents international economic inequality. Violent familial socialization processes, particularly harsh punishment of children, may be reflective of different socioeconomic standings across different nations (Runyan et al., 2010). Economic disadvantage may positively influence criminal behavior (Farrington, 2003; Lipsey & Derzon, 1998). And GDP is correlated with murder rates (Gartner, 1993). These facts suggest the possibility of variation in criminal behavior that could be explained through social class differences. Because the present study examines national context effects, *GDP* was used to control for the effect of national socioeconomic influences on criminal behavior. This variable is used in both ordinary least squares and multilevel modeling regression analyses. Due to *GDP* being a continuous variable, the scale was centered on the grand-mean of all individual cases for the MLM regression analysis. This variable is for a level-2 control in multilevel modeling regression analysis.

Analyses

Before conducting regression analyses to test the two main hypotheses, two types of statistical tests were performed to examine the "norms of violence" thesis. T-tests were used to examine the extent to which violent socialization differs among nations with (1) laws prohibiting the use of physical discipline and (2) laws prohibiting the use of the death penalty. Bivariate correlations were used to examine the degree to which homicide rates were associated with violent socialization.

T-tests

An independent samples *t*-test will be used to test whether or not violent socialization processes are part of violent norms within a nation. Two *t*-tests will be performed on violent socialization: one *t*-test comparing nations with laws prohibiting the use of physical discipline of children to nations with no such laws, and one *t*-test comparing nations with laws abolishing the use of the death penalty to nations without these laws. The results of the *t*-test will show the average level of violent socialization processes by nations with each of these laws. The results will also show whether or not the averages between groups significantly differ. If violent socialization processes significantly differ between nations with laws banning these two types of violence and nations without such law, the results of the *t*-tests will provide some support in favor of norms of violence occurring within a context.

Bivariate Correlations

Pearson product moment correlation coefficient was examined to further analyze the norms of violence thesis. According to this thesis, the correlation coefficient should show (1) significant correlations between laws prohibiting physical discipline of children and violent socialization, with decreased violent socialization in nations that prohibit the use of physical discipline on children; (2) significant correlations between laws abolishing the death penalty and violent socialization, with decreased violent socialization in nations that have abolished the death penalty; and (3) homicide rates being significantly, positively associated with violent socialization, such that nations with high national-level homicide rates will have increased levels of violent socialization. These three predictions are expected to support the norms of violence thesis: if violent socialization processes are significantly negatively correlated with national laws banning these two types of violence, the results of the *t*-tests will provide additional support in favor of norms of violence occurring within a context. Tables 4.6–8 display the results of the bivariate correlations among all the variables.

Multilevel Modeling Regression Analysis

To account for the degree to which group-level similarities in familial socialization processes may occur within the same nation (i.e., clustering of youth via socialization processes), as well as differences across nations, multilevel modeling regression analysis is necessary (Bickel, 2007; Luke, 2004; Raudenbush & Bryk, 2002). Multilevel modeling regression analysis accounts for the effects of clustering within the same nation while estimating a relationship across different nations. Multilevel modeling regression also tests for significant variation among groups. In order to determine if there is significant variation in violent socialization processes across different nations and if this variation significantly contributes to differences in criminal behavior cross-nationally, multilevel modeling regression (MLM) will be used to test all three hypotheses. But, MLM will be used to fully test the third hypothesis H_3: *criminal behavior will significantly vary nation to nation as a function of violent socialization processes, serving within a context of norms of violence.*

MLM regression techniques were designed to separate individual and group-level effects on the dependent variable (Bryk & Raudenbush, 1992; Goldstein, 1988; Jones & Subramanian, 2019). The respondents are "nested" within nations. As stated previously, respondents within the same nation may be exposed to similar standards in socialization processes (e.g., see Keller, Otto, Lamm, Yovsi, & Kartner, 2008; Levinson, 1989), a context in which these respondents are more similar to each other compared to respondents from different nations. This context could produce more homogeneous experiences. In other words, because socialization processes vary across different nations (Urquiza & Goodlin-Jones, 1994), youth within the same nation may have comparable socialization experiences compared to youth from different nations, creating a contextual effect (Jones & Subramanian, 2019) in which the respondents from the same nation cluster together.

Therefore, using Ordinary Least Square (OLS) regression alone could be problematic. OLS regression assumes cases are statistically independent (Bryk & Raudenbush, 1992) and measurement error for each predictor variable in the model is independent and unrelated (Hamilton, 1992). Because the data in the IDVS were collected as groups of students within the same college/university then aggregated by nation (Straus, 2009) and compiled together into a single dataset, the data is considered hierarchical data. Assumptions of independence, then, are violated in the presence of hierarchical data. This violation can increase the probability of rejecting a null hypothesis (Hamilton, 1992) because error terms for similar cases may be correlated (Jones & Subramanian,

2019; Luke, 2004). As such, individual cases within each of the nations are not fully independent. Further, OLS regression cannot examine contextual effects and, alone, is not appropriate for testing the proposed norms of violence thesis. To address the possibility of clustering within nations, multilevel modeling regression analysis becomes an important tool to control for different contextual effects (Bickel, 2007; Jones & Subramanian, 2019; Luke, 2004) and disentangle possible group-level similarities in socialization process both within and between nations.

MLM will show national-level averages in youth criminal behavior while testing for variation due to violent socialization processes, net of controls, and accounting for the nesting of data. MLM regression allows for estimating the effects of the predictor variables on the outcome variable at both the individual and group level simultaneously (Jones & Subramanian, 2019; Raudenbush & Byrk, 1986). The MLM regression analysis is expected to reveal significant variation in criminal behavior both within and between the different nations, and violent socialization, within this context, will significantly predict criminal behavior. This prediction is also based on analysis of the correlations between the main level-2 predictor variable (i.e., violent socialization in the nation) and youth criminal behavior. As seen in Table 4.6, these two variables are significantly correlated.

There are a small number of nations for the level-2 analysis (n = 32) in the present study, which would typically be expected to lack sufficient statistical power to detect the effects of violent socialization criminal behavior (Hayes, 2006; Lipsey, 1990). However, analysis of the correlations for the level-2 sample size (see Table 4.4) and exploration of the regression parameter estimates (i.e., intercept and slope), described in the next chapter, suggest that the expected effect sizes should be large enough to detect a statistically significant relationship between violent socialization in the nation and youth criminal behavior.

Table 4.6 Correlations between Level-2 Predictor Variables (n = 32) and Criminal Behavior (for t-tests and MLM Level-2)

Variables	*1*	*2*	*3*	*4*	*5*	*6*	*7*
violent socialization	–						
vscommunity	.36*	–					
discipline	−.36*	−.06**	–				
death penalty	−.36*	−.16**	.51**	–			
homicide rate	.04**	.04**	−.07**	−.17**	–		
GDP	−.47**	−.14**	−.33**	.09**	−.29**	–	
criminal behavior	.36**	.46**	−.03**	−.08**	.02**	.00	–

** p ≤ 0.01 * p ≤ 0.05

Table 4.7 Correlations between Level-1 Predictor Variables (n = 12,640) and Criminal Behavior (for OLS and MLM Level-1)

Variables	*1*	*2*	*3*	*4*	*5*	*6*	*7*	*8*	*9*	*10*
violent comm	–									
violent family	.51**	–								
attachment	−.26**	−.42**	–							
self-control	−.33**	−.38**	.42**	–						
peer crime	.18**	.20**	−.14**	−.25**	–					
gender	.27**	.13**	−.09**	−.17**	.09**	–				
age	.01	.03**	−.08**	.03**	.08	.09**	–			
ses	−.08**	−.11**	.13**	.00	.03**	.04**	−.04**	–		
social desire	−.19**	−.22**	.21**	.43**	−.29**	−.03**	.03**	−.02*	–	
criminal behavior	.36**	.44**	−.32**	−.42**	.18**	.23**	.04**	.02*	−.28**	–

** $p \leq 0.01$ * $p \leq 0.05$

Ordinary Least Squares Regression

Ordinary Least Squares regression (OLS) will be performed on data for each individual nation in order to compare nation-to-nation results. OLS regression analysis will also test the first two hypotheses, except by each nation separately. OLS regression will provide information about the strength and direction of these relationships for each individual nation. A higher level of violent socialization is expected to be significantly associated with more youth criminal behavior. This finding is expected to hold true even in the presence of protective factors: stronger attachments and higher self-control. As seen in Table 4.7, each of these variables is significantly correlated to youth criminal behavior.

OLS regression will also be used to further test the third hypothesis (H_3), in part, to explore the specific variation in youth criminal behavior across nations due to violent socialization processes. The results are expected to demonstrate that higher levels of *violent socialization* are significantly associated with more youth criminal behavior but that this association will be different for each nation. However, this finding is expected among only the nations with at least 150 respondents (Fowler, 2009) because otherwise, there may not be sufficient statistical power to detect significant effects among the variables unless the effect is very large (Lipsey, 1990). For example, violent socializations are not expected to significantly predict criminal behavior among the respondents in Iran due to the limited number of cases (n = 99).

Notes

1 This measure was translated for each country as one days' wage for skilled manual labor (Straus, personal communication, December 13, 2011).

2 Two measures in this scale, "my parents helped me when I had trouble understanding something" (under helping) and "my parents did not care if I did things like shoplifting (under supervising), were not available in the original data of the IDVS (see Straus, Hamby, Boney-McCoy, & Sugarman, 2010) and therefore were not used in this study.

Chapter 5

Analyzing Norms of Violence

To begin the preliminary analysis to examine the "norms of violence" thesis, first the relationship between violent socialization and youth criminal behavior needs to be established. If this relationship exists, then the data need to be examined to determine whether or not there are associations between the different manifestations of violence within the nations.

The Overlap of Violence

The bivariate correlations, shown in Tables 4.6 through 5.1, indicate a significant, positive relationship between violent socialization and youth criminal behavior. For violent socialization in the community, the relationship ranges from weakly moderate ($r=0.32$, $p<0.01$) at the individual level (among all respondents within one nation) to moderate ($r=0.46$, $p<0.01$) at the aggregate level (national level means). Violent familial socialization holds a moderate relationship with youth criminal behavior ($r=0.44$, $p<0.01$). And when looking at overall violent socialization at national level averages, the relationship is also moderate ($r=0.46$, $p<0.01$). This indicates that as more violent socialization occurs, there is more youth criminal behavior.

To continue this preliminary analysis of the norms of violence thesis, the bivariate correlations indicate a significant, negative relationship between the legal measures of violence for the nations and youth criminal behavior (see Table 4.6). This is interpreted as where the legal measures of violence are *not* present in the nations, youth criminal behavior decreases. Specifically, in the nations where there are laws prohibiting the use of physical punishment on children, youth criminal behavior significantly decreases ($r=-0.03$, $p<0.05$). The same is true of nations with laws abolishing the use of the death penalty ($r=-0.08$, $p<0.05$). And finally, in the nations in which the homicide rates increase, youth criminal behavior also increases ($r=0.04$, $p<0.01$). Now comparing violent socialization processes at the aggregate level and these nation-based legal measures of violence, there is a significant negative relationship. For aggregate violent socialization process, the relationship is moderate ($r=-0.36$, $p<0.05$) for both *discipline* and *death penalty*. For violent communal socialization

Table 5.1 Correlations Between All Variables and Criminal Behavior

	1	*2*	*3*	*4*	*5*	*6*	*7*	*8*	*9*	*10*	*11*	*12*	*13_*	*14*	*15*	*16*
violent socialization	–															
vscommunity	.21	–														
discipline	−.36*	−.02*	–													
death penalty	−.36*	−.10**	.51**	–												
homicide rate	.29	.04**	−.17**	−.07**	–											
GDP	−.47**	−.12**	-.33**	−.09**	−.29**	–										
violent comm	.36*	−.82**	−.06**	.16**	−.12**	−.14**	–									
violent family	.91**	.51**	−.08**	−.17**	.05**	−.13*	.38*	–								
attachment	−.44*	−.26**	−.10**	.12**	.02**	.19**	−.40**	−.42**	–							
self- control	−.15	−.33**	−.06**	.14**	.01	.24**	−.41**	−.38**	.42**	–						
peer crime	.33	.18**	−.01	−.11**	−.04**	−.08**	.22**	.20**	−.14**	−.25**	–					
gender	−.03	.27**	−.03**	.09**	.03**	−.05**	−.21**	.13**	.09**	.17**	−.09**	–				
age	−.05	.01	.05**	.05**	−.06**	−.02**	.03**	.03**	−.08**	.03**	.01	−.09**	–			
ses	−.05	−.08**	−.01	.01	.01	.01**	−.11**	−.11**	.13**	.00	.03**	−.04**	−.04**	–		
socialdesire	−.04	.19**	−.07**	.06**	.10**	.01	−.23**	−.22**	−.21**	.43**	−29**	−.03**	.03**	−.02**	–	
criminal behavior	.46**	.46**	−.08**	−.02**	.05**	.36**	.32**	.44**	−.32**	.42**	.18**	−.23**	.04**	.02*	−.02*	–

**p≤0.01 * p≤0.05

processes, the relationships are weak: (*discipline*=-0.06, $p<0.05$; *death penalty*= −0.16, $p<0.05$).

While many of these relationships are weak, the bivariate analyses indicate that relationships between these variables exist and, as predicted, are consistent with the propositions of the norms of violence thesis. In countries where there are laws prohibiting the use of violence within social control, both violent socialization and youth criminal behavior significantly decrease. It is important to also compare the levels of violence in each nation. The results of the *t*-tests are shown in Figures 5.1 and 5.2. Figure 5.1 shows the average level of violent socialization scores among nations with and without laws prohibiting physical discipline on children. Figure 5.2 shows the average level of violent socialization scores among nations with and without the death penalty.

First looking at laws prohibiting the use of physical discipline on children (Figure 5.1), among these 24 nations the average violent socialization score was 14.25, while the average violent socialization score among the 8 nations with no such legal prohibitions on the use of physical discipline was 15.875. There are significant differences in violent socialization processes according to the presence or absence of anti-physical discipline laws ($t=4.687$, $p<0.05$).

A *t*-test was also used to test whether or not violent socialization significantly differs among nations that have abolished the use of the death penalty and nations with no such prohibition (Figure 5.2). The average violent socialization score for the 19 nations with laws prohibiting the use of the death penalty was 13.5263. The average violent socialization score among the 12 nations that still use the death

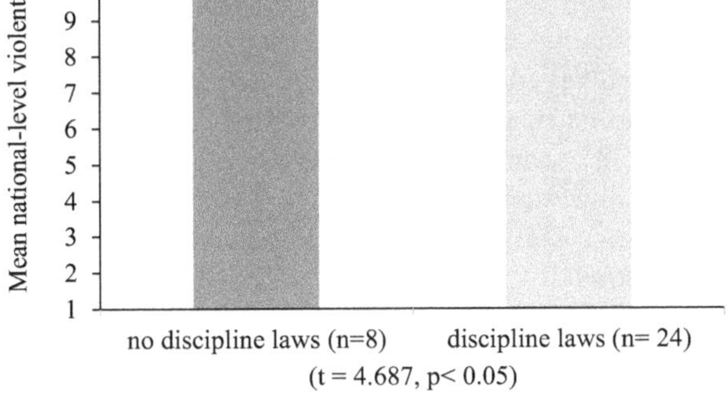

Figure 5.1 Average level of violent socialization scores among nations with & without laws prohibiting physical discipline on children

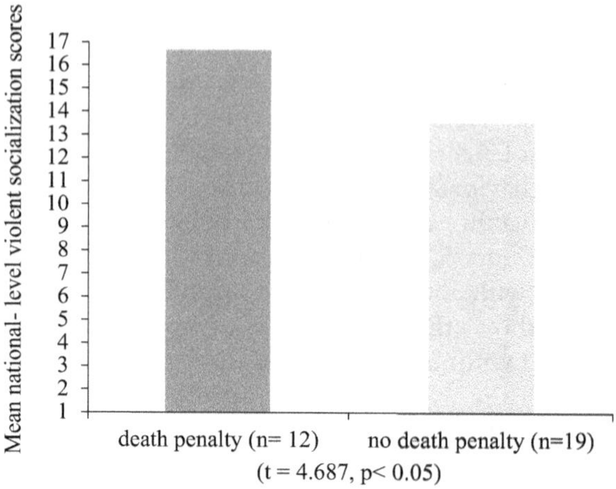

Figure 5.2 Average level of violent socialization scores among nations with & without the death penalty

penalty as a form of criminal sanctioning was 16.6667. The results of this *t*-test indicate there are significant differences in violent socialization processes according to the presence or absence of the death penalty laws ($t=2.218$, $p<0.05$).

Based on the results of these two t-tests, there appears to be some preliminary support favoring the norms of violence thesis. Violent socialization processes appear to be more frequent in nations favoring violence: nationally supported violence against children, in the form of physical discipline, and state-sanctioned homicide, via the death penalty. Explained through the norms of violence thesis, some nations associate violence as a normative response to conflict more so than other nations. Some nations may hold formal norms, embedded in laws, which sanction violence-based responses while other nations have embraced more of a non-violent approach.

Overall, this preliminary analysis reveals that violence against others, in a general sense, tends to be more prevalent in some nations compared to other nations. The results of these preliminary analyses indicate further investigation is warranted to test this premise. To continue testing the norms of violence thesis, MLM regression analysis is necessary to determine whether or not there is an association between violent socialization and criminal behavior while controlling for other contributing factors.

The Context of Living in Violence

As outlined earlier, youth living in the same nation may cluster together based on similarities in socialization experiences. Therefore, in the present study, there may be a contextual effect of violent socialization processes within each of the 32 nations in the IDVS. In some nations, violence may be part of the normative experiences for the youth living in that nation. In this sense, criminal behavior may significantly vary nation to nation as a function of violent socialization processes, serving within a context of norms of violence. To address this issue of possible group-level similarities by nation, multilevel modeling regression analysis (MLM) controls for different contextual effects within and between groups (Bickel, 2007; Luke, 2004). Multilevel modeling regression analysis effectively models the impact of differences at a national level on individual outcomes. Table 5.2 lists the results from fitting the preliminary multilevel models to self-reported criminal behavior regressed on level-1 and level-2 main predictors.

The estimated intraclass correlation coefficient (ICC), calculated as $p = T_{00} / \sigma^2 + T_{00}$ from Model 0 in Table 5.2,[1] is used as a parameter estimate to determine the proportion of total variance that accounts for the clustering (Hayes, 2006) of violent socialization processes for each nation. The ICC, listed in Table 5.2, indicates that 5.7% of the variation in criminal behavior is between nations, showing some clustering of criminal behavior between nations. Although most of the variation in youth criminal behavior is explained by individual-level factors (94.3%), MLM is still an important tool to disentangle possible contextual effects.

Transnational Crime

To begin the analyses, exploratory multilevel models were used to determine the degree to which criminal behavior varies among the nations in the IDVS (i.e., the "unconditional model"), the association between a contextual effect of violent socialization processes and criminal behavior (i.e., "means as outcome model"), and the influence of violent family socialization, attachments, and self-control on criminal behavior (i.e., "random coefficient models").

The unconditional model in Table 5.2, Model 0, a model containing no predictors (Wang, 1998) that is used to determine the amount of variation in criminal behavior within and between nations, models the observed score for individual *i* in country *j* as the sum of an overall average score for criminal behavior across all nations, plus two residuals (one representing deviations between each nation average criminal behavior score and the mean for all countries, and the other residual representing the deviation in criminal behavior between individual *i* and his or her respective national mean). The composite equation for this model is specified as:

$$Y_{ij} = \gamma_{00} + [u_{0j} + r_{ij}].$$

Results from fitting this unconditional model indicate that the predicted mean score for criminal behavior, across all nations, is estimated at an average of

Table 5.2 Results from Fitting the Preliminary Multilevel Models to Self-Reported Criminal Behavior Regressed on Level-1 and Level-2 Main Predictors (n of College Students = 12,640; n of Nations = 32)

		Model 0	*Model 1*	*Model 2a*	*Model 2b*	*Model 3*
Fixed Effects						
Intercept	γ_{00}	5.604***	5.627***	5.646***	5.634***	5.638***
vscommunity	γ_{01}		0.375***			0.199***
vsfamily	γ_{10}			0.328***	0.314***	0.245***
Variance Components (Random Effects)						
Level-1: Within	σ^2	3.985***	3.503***	3.272***	3.260***	3.157***
Level-2: Between	T_{00}	0.214***	0.121***	0.096***	0.100***	0.093***
	T_{01}				0.014**	0.013**
	T_{11}				0.002*	0.002*
Interclass Correlation	5.7%					
Pseudo-R²						
% within nation			12.1	17.8	20.8	20.8
% between nations			43.5	55.1	53.3	56.5
Goodness of Fit Statistics						
2LL		66148.608	64119.159	63046.525	63002.713	62497.314
AIC		66154.608	64127.159	63054.525	63014.713	62511.314
BIC		66177.583	64157.792	63085.158	63060.663	62106.604

*** $p<0.001$ **$p<0.01$ *$p<0.05$

about 5.6 points (γ_{00} = 5.604, p > 0.001) on a scale ranging from 4 points to 16 points. The unconditional model also shows that there is significant variation in criminal behavior scores both within each nation ($\sigma^2 = 3.985$, $p < .001$) and between the different nations ($T_{00} = 0.214$, $p < .001$) with about 18 times more variation in criminal behavior scores within each nation compared to between the different nations. To understand if there is a contextual effect of violent socialization, the preliminary analysis needs to continue to examine if criminal behavior continues to significantly vary while accounting for the contextual effect of violent socialization.

Violent Socialization as a Contextual Effect

Violent socialization in the community (*vscommunity*), the main level-2 predictor, is added to the unconditional model in the means as outcome model, Model 1 (see Table 5.2). This model examines if the effect of violent socialization at the national level is associated with *criminal behavior.* The equation for the full means as outcome model is specified as:

$$Y_{ij} = [\gamma_{00} + \gamma_{01}\ vscommunity_j] + [u_{0j} + r_{ij}].$$

This model estimates that nations with mean levels of violent socialization average criminal behavior scores of about 5.6 points (γ_{00} = 5.627, $p < 0.001$) when accounting for the effect of violent socialization in the community. Higher levels of national violent socialization tend to significantly increase criminal behavior scores, by an estimated 0.38 points for each 1 increase in the *vscommunity* scale (γ_{01} = 0.375, $p < .001$). The predicted criminal behavior score for the prototypical respondent who experienced violent socialization in the community is approximately 6 points ($\gamma_{00} + \gamma_{01}$). So, the respondents who experienced violent socialization in the community tended to report more criminal behavior compared to respondents who did not experience violent socialization processes in the community. This result begins to show preliminary support for the first hypothesis: youth in nations that use violent socialization processes tend to engage in more criminal behavior.

The results from fitting Model 1 indicate that violent socialization in the community alone explains about 12% of the variation in criminal behavior within the same nation and about 43.5% between the different nations (i.e., Pseudo-R^2). Further, in this model, after controlling for violent socialization in the community, not only do estimated criminal behavior scores within nations continue to significantly vary ($\sigma^2 = 3.503$, $p < .001$), there also continues to be significant differences in criminal behavior scores across different nations ($T_{00} = 0.121$, $p < .001$). The third hypothesis, in part, is initially supported, in that criminal behavior varies from nation to nation due to violent socialization processes. However, because the null hypothesis is rejected by the intercept variance ($T_{00} = 0.121$, $p < .001$), there still may be an additional "explainable" variation that accounts for criminal behavior. Hence, how much variation in criminal behavior can be accounted for by respondents' individual circumstances within their individual families?

Violent Socialization within the Family

To answer this question, the random coefficient models (models 2a and 2b in Table 5.2) are models adding respondents' experiences of violent socialization within their individual families, one at a time, as fixed effects and random effects, to the unconditional model. The present study is primarily testing the effects of violent socialization processes on criminal behavior, rather than complicate the model with multiple different random effects. This analysis is necessary to examine the degree to which criminal behavior varies within each nation when accounting for the effects of the level-1 variable. General linear hypothesis tests, used to determine which model best fits the data, indicate that the overall best-fitting model is Model 2b. (The general linear hypothesis tests are shown in Table 7.1 in Appendix A.) The equation for the full random coefficient model is

$$Y_{ij} = [\gamma_{00} + \gamma_{10}\ vsfamily] + [u_{0j} + u_{1j}\ vsfamily + r_{ij}].$$

Model 2b shows that, on average, increases in violent familial socialization are significantly associated with increases in individual criminal behavior scores. Criminal behavior scores for respondents with mean levels of violent familial socialization are estimated at 5.6 points ($\gamma_{00} = 5.634$, $p < 0.001$). Higher levels of violent familial socialization tend to significantly increase criminal behavior scores, by an estimated 0.31 points for each 1 point increase on the violent familial socialization scale on average ($\gamma_{01} = 0.314$, $p < 0.001$). The predicted criminal behavior score for the prototypical respondent who experienced violent familial socialization is approximately 6.9 points (γ_{01} + constant). The respondents who experienced violent family socialization tended to report more criminal behavior compared to respondents who did not experience violent familial socialization processes. This model now explains about 21% of the variation in criminal behavior within the same nation and about 53.3% between the different nations (i.e., Pseudo-R^2). This result begins to show preliminary support for the second hypothesis: youth from families that use violent socialization processes tend to engage in more criminal behavior. But in order to provide valid support this hypothesis, protective factors of social controls need to be included in the model.

Violent Socialization and Crime

Given the results of the general linear hypothesis test, models 1 and 2b were combined to explore the effects of both the level-1 and level-2 predictor variables together on youth criminal behavior scores. This model (Model 3) allows for an examination of the degree to which violent socialization processes, as a whole, may be associated with youth criminal behavior. The final multilevel model consists of three equations: the individual-level model, the contextual effect model, and the composite model. These equations are specified as:

Level-1:

$$\text{criminal behavio } r_{ij} = \beta_{0j} + \beta_{1j}\text{ vs family} + u_{0j} + u_{1j}\text{ vs family}]\, r_{ij},$$

$$\text{where } r \sim N\left(0, \sigma^2\right)$$

Level-2:

$$\beta_{0j} = \gamma_{00} + \gamma_{01}\mathit{community}_j + \mathrm{u}_{0j}$$

$$\beta_{1j} = \gamma_{10}$$

$$\mathit{where}\ \mathrm{u}_{0j} \sim N\ (0, \mathrm{T}_{00})$$

Composite:

$$\mathit{criminal\ behavior}_{ij} = [\gamma_{00} + \gamma_{01}\mathit{vscommunity}_j + \gamma_{10}\ \mathit{vsfamily}_{ij}] + [u_{0j} + u_{1j}\ \mathit{vsfamily} + \mathrm{r}_{ij}]].$$

In Model 3, the explanatory power of the model improves. The pseudo-R^2 indicates that violent socialization, as a whole, explains about 21% of the variation in youth criminal behavior scores within the same nation, while these same variables explain 56.5% of the variation in youth criminal behavior scores across the different nations. This finding was expected. The variables together would better explain variance in youth criminal behavior given that each variable is measured at a different level and represents a unique level-based construct for each of the levels in the model. Individual families are nested within nations, but have varying methods in which to socialize their youth. As discussed previously, nations vary in cultural practices of socialization for youth. Therefore, the individual and group level variables together better explain youth criminal behavior transnationally.

Further, after controlling for violent socialization at the group and individual level, not only do estimated youth criminal behavior scores within nations continue to significantly vary ($\sigma^2=3.157$, $p < .001$), there also continues to be significant differences in youth criminal behavior scores across different nations ($T_{00}=0.093$, $p<.001$). Higher levels of violent socialization in the community tend to significantly increase youth criminal behavior scores. For each 1 point increase on the violent socialization in the community scale, mean youth criminal behavior scores increase by an estimated 0.20 points for ($\gamma_{01}=0.199$, $p<0.001$) on average, net of violent familial socialization. This is also true of higher levels of violent familial socialization: mean youth criminal behavior scores tend to increase by an estimated 0.25 points, on average, for each 1 point increase on the violent familial socialization scale ($\gamma_{10}=0.245$, $p<0.001$) net of violent socialization in the community. The prototypical mean youth criminal behavior score for youth who experience both manifestations of violent socialization is about 6 points, on average ($\gamma_{00}+\gamma_{01}+\gamma_{10}$). Model 3 further shows that violent socialization within individual families continued to be variable ($T_{11}=0.002$, $p < .05$) and this effect varies in nations with different mean youth criminal behavior scores ($T_{01} = 0.013$, $p < .01$).

Examining all exploratory multilevel models together (Models 1–3), the effects for both individual familial socialization processes and violent socialization occurring within communities seems to indicate that youth criminal behavior is significantly explained through a context in which socialization processes occur within nations. This result further shows support for the first and second hypotheses. It also begins to show support for the norms of violence thesis: when youth are exposed to violent socialization processes in their families and communities, these ineffective socialization processes increase youth criminal behavior. Violence may be normalized and accepted more so than if youth experience only one type of violent socialization. For example, while the family may normalize the use of violence as a means to control youth behavior, youth could be exposed to communities within their nation that do not practice violent socialization processes. This may communicate to youth that certain socialization practices are deviant despite the normalization of such practices within their family. As a result, these youth may be less inclined to engage in criminal behavior.

But, in order to provide valid support to this thesis, this model needs to account for the effect of other theoretical explanations for youth criminal behavior. Further, variation in youth criminal behavior, at least across different nations, is better explained through a context in which violent socialization may be more prevalent within certain nations while other nations embrace more effective methods of socialization. In other words, when including both the level-1 and level-2 main predictor variables, the international pseudo-R^2 in model 3 increases by more than 25% over Model 1 (contextual effect only) and more than 5% over both Model 2 (individual circumstances only) for the between-nation variance components. However, the null hypothesis is rejected by the intercept variance ($T_{00}=0.093$, $p<0.001$) so additional models need to test control variables to look for additional "explainable" variation to account for youth criminal behavior scores. In order to provide valid support to the norms of violence thesis, the taxonomy of models needs to account for the effect of other theoretical explanations for youth criminal behavior.

Other Theoretical Explanations for Youth Criminal Behavior

As discussed previously, there are well-supported theories of crime in the current literature. These theories include social control, learning, and culture of violence. In order to demonstrate support for the norms of violence thesis, beyond the scope of these theories, the main constructs of these other theories need to be controlled for in the model. Failure to include other theoretical control variables associated with youth criminal behavior could lend the possibility of spuriousness. Each model in the taxonomy of models is fitted as a progressively more complex multilevel model, by adding each competing theoretical variable to the model. The results of these taxonomies are presented in Table 5.3.

Social Control

The protective factors of social control with the most imperial validity within criminological theories are attachments within the family and individual self-control. Each of these variables are included within Model 4 (Table 5.3). In this model, the effects of violent socialization on youth criminal behavior remain constant even in the presence of attachments and self-control. Violent socialization continues to be significantly associated with increases in criminal behavior scores even when controlling for attachment and self-control, both in the community ($\gamma_{01}=0.152$, $p<0.001$) and within families ($\gamma_{10}=0.152$, $p<0.001$). Higher levels of national-level violent socialization tends to significantly increase criminal behavior scores, by an estimated 0.38 points for each 1 point increase in violent socialization in the community (γ_{01} = 0.375, $p < .001$) on average, net of violent familial socialization and other controls. The predicted mean youth criminal behavior score for the prototypical respondent with average attachments and self-control but experienced violent socialization both in the community and family is approximately 6 points ($\gamma_{00}+\gamma_{01}+\gamma_{10}+\gamma_{20+}\gamma_{30}$), on average.

When partitioning the variance components, Model 4 shows that approximately 28% of the variation in youth criminal behavior within the same nation (Pseudo-$R^2=28.7$) can be explained by both the violent socialization and social control variables. These same variables explain about 32% of the variation in youth criminal behavior between different nations (Pseudo-$R^2=32.2$). Model 4 offers more explanatory power in mean youth criminal behavior over Model 3, both within nations and between the different nations. This result can be explained as more variables in the regression model would explain more youth criminal behavior. But, the overall results do not support the social control

Table 5.3 Results from Fitting the Taxonomy of Multilevel Models to Self-Reported Youth Criminal Behavior Regressed on Level-1 and Level-2 Predictors (n of Respondents = 12,640; n of Nations = 32)

		Model 4	*Model 5*	*Model 6*	*Model 7*	*Model 8*	*Model 9*	*Model 10*	*Model 11*	*Model 12*
Fixed Effects										
Intercept	γ_{00}	5.597***	5.454***	5.452***	5.452***	5.638***	5.457***	5.393***	5.213***	5.287***
vsfamily	γ_{10}	0.152***	0.236***	0.246***	0.246***	0.250***	0.250***	0.153***	0.150*	0.150***
attachment	γ_{20}	−0.099***						−0.103***	−0.102***	−0.102***
self-control	γ_{30}	−0.226***						−0.179***	−0.180***	−0.181***
peer	γ_{40}		0.341***					0.092**	0.100**	0.098**
gender	γ_{50}			0.645***	0.642***		0.622***	0.567***	0.565***	0.565**
age	γ_{60}				0.006		0.009	0.018**	0.019**	0.020**
ses	γ_{70}					0.144**	0.126***	0.135**	0.136***	0.136***
socdesire	γ_{80}							−0.047***	−0.048***	−0.049***
Vscommunity	γ_{01}	0.152***	0.188***	0.156***	0.156***	0.201***	0.160***	0.113***	0.112***	0.111***
discipline	γ_{02}								0.172	0.179
death penalty	γ_{03}								0.376**	0.394**
homicide	γ_{04}								0.012*	0.011*
GDP	γ_{05}									−0.022~
Variance Components (Random Effects)										
Level-1: Within	σ^2	2.877***	3.131***	3.078***	3.078***	3.138***	3.063***	2.763***	2.769***	2.768***
Level-2: Between	T_{00}	0.145***	0.091***	0.080*****	0.080**	0.091***	0.078**	0.106***	0.124***	0.113**
	T_{01}	0.009*	0.002**	0.011**	0.011**	0.013**	0.011**	0.011**	0.011*	0.011*
	T_{11}	0.002*	0.002**	0.002*	0.002*	0.002*	0.002*	0.002**	0.002*	0.002*
Pseudo-R²										
% reduction within		27.8	21.4	22.8	22.8	31.2	23.1	30.7	30.5	30.5
% reduction between		32.2	57.5	62.6	62.6	57.5	63.6	50.5	42.1	47.2
Goodness of Fit Statistics										
2LL		49329.302	62364.691	62097.294	62174.561	62401.082	62021.228	48819.712	48146.606	48181.639
AIC		49347.302	62380.691	62113.294	62114.306	62417.082	62041.228	48847.712	48180.606	48181.694
BIC		49414.304	62441.958	62174.561	62183.231	62478.348	62117.812	48951.936	48306.924	48315.387

*** p<0.001 **p<0.01 *p<0.05 ~p<0.10

variables as preventative measures for youth criminal behavior. Although both higher levels of attachments (γ_{20}=-0.099, $p<0.001$) and self-control (γ_{30}=-0.226, $p<0.001$) tend to significantly reduce mean youth criminal behavior, the predicted mean youth criminal behavior score for the prototypical respondents remains the same as Model 3. If attachment and self-control significantly reduced youth criminal behavior, the predicted mean youth criminal behavior score across nations would be lower in Model 4 compared to Model 3. Thus, in the presence of violent socialization, effective social control has virtually no preventative effect.

The results from Model 4 show further support for the first and second hypotheses. Youth who experience violent socialization processes engage in more criminal behavior, even in the presence of effective social control markers, compared to youth from communities and families that do not use violent socialization processes. Model 4 continues to offer support for the norms of violence thesis: when youth are exposed to violent socialization processes in their families and communities, these ineffective socialization processes increase youth criminal behavior. The strength of normalized and accepted violence may be so powerful that known protective factors have no preventative effect. Further, there is continued support for the third hypothesis: youth criminal behavior significantly varies from nation to nation as a function of violent socialization processes. After controlling for violent socialization at the group and individual level, the estimated youth criminal behavior scores within nations continue to significantly vary (σ^2=2.877, $p < .001$) and differences in youth criminal behavior scores across different nations continue to be significant (T_{00}=0.145, $p<.001$). And, with these families nested within nations, the effect of violent familial socialization on youth criminal behavior significantly varies in nations with different mean youth criminal behavior scores (T_{01} = 0.009, $p < .05$). Overall, this model offers on-going support of a context of norms of violence, in which criminal behavior varies transnationally as a function of violent socialization processes. Socialization processes, used to control youth behavior, are less effective within nations that embrace a context favoring violence to resolve conflict. The variance in hegemonic cultural contexts of violence spill over from the nation to individual families, impacting the methods used to control youth behavior. However, the findings are not conclusive unless other prominent theories of crime can be ruled out.

Learning

In order to discount the impact of youth learning criminal behavior from peers, a variable representing learning theory is included in the taxonomy of models. Model 5 (Table 5.3) presents the results. In this model, the effects of violent socialization on youth criminal behavior remain constant even in the presence of attachments and self-control. Violent socialization continues to be significantly associated with increases in youth criminal behavior scores even when controlling for peers' criminal behavior, both in the community and within families. Higher levels of national-level violent socialization tend to significantly increase youth criminal behavior scores, by an estimated 0.19 points for each 1 point increase in violent socialization in the community ($\gamma_{01}=0.188$, $p<0.001$) on average, net of violent familial socialization. Higher levels of violent familial socialization also tend to significantly increase youth criminal behavior scores, by an estimated 0.19 points for each 1 point increase in violent familial socialization ($\gamma_{10}=0.236$, $p<0.001$) on average, net of violent socialization in the community. The predicted mean youth criminal behavior score for the prototypical respondent who experienced violent socialization both in the community and family and has peers who engage in the criminal behavior ($\gamma_{40}=0.341$, $p<0.001$) is approximately 6.2 points ($\gamma_{00}+\gamma_{01}+\gamma_{10}+\gamma_{40}$), on average.

Partitioning of the variance components, Model 5 shows that approximately 21% of the variation in youth criminal behavior within the same nation (Pseudo-$R^2=21.4$) can be explained by both the violent socialization and social control variables. These same variables explain about 57% of the variation in youth criminal behavior between different nations (Pseudo-$R^2=57.4$). Model 5 offers slightly more explanatory power over Model 4in mean youth criminal behavior between the different nations, with an approximate 75% increase in the Pseudo- R^2. This result can be explained by the fact that peers are members of the community and these peers may engage violent socialization. While not tested in the present study, peers may engage in criminal behavior because they experienced their own violent socialization. This violent socialization may occur within the context of the nation as a normative process, both in the community and within individual families. Violent socialization within individual families continues to be variable ($T_{11}=0.002$, $p < .01$) and this effect varies in nations with different mean youth criminal behavior scores ($T_{01} = 0.002$, $p < .01$).

The results of Model 5 do not lend substantive support for learning theories over the norms of violence thesis. If peers' criminal behavior was a considerable factor contributing to the perpetration of youth criminal behavior, the predicted mean youth criminal score would significantly increase over Model 4. It did not. Further, after controlling for violent socialization and peer criminal behavior, the estimated youth criminal behavior scores within nations continue to significantly vary ($\sigma^2=3.131$, $p < .001$) and differences in youth criminal behavior scores across different nations continue to be significant ($T_{00}=0.091$, $p<.001$). When youth have experienced violent socialization, the influence of their peers teaching them to engage in criminal behavior has little effect. These results, from Model 5, show further support for the first and second hypotheses. Youth who experience violent socialization processes engage in more criminal behavior. The criminal behavior may be amplified when youth have peers who engage in criminal behavior, but the experiences with violence still lend for more criminal behavior among youth, particularly compared to the youth who have not experienced violent socialization processes.

Model 5 continues to offer support for the norms of violence thesis: when youth are exposed to violent socialization processes in their families and communities ($\gamma_{10+}\gamma_{01}$), these ineffective socialization processes increase youth criminal behavior and the increases are more profound than only having peers who engage in criminal behavior (γ_{04}). The normalcy of violence may be so infiltrated within nations that the collective conscious does not recognize certain behaviors and interactions as violence. These results offer continued support for the third hypothesis: youth criminal behavior significantly varies from nation to nation as a function of violent socialization processes. While this model offers additional support for a context of norms of violence, the culture of violence needs to be tested.

Culture of Violence

Models 6–9 show youth criminal behavior regressed on violent socialization, including the effects of various concepts associated with culture of violence theories: gender, age, and socioeconomic status. In each model, violent socialization continues to be significantly associated with increases in youth criminal behavior scores even when controlling for gender and socioeconomic status.

Gender. Model 6 shows the effect of gender when included in the regression model. In this model, higher levels of national-level violent socialization tend to significantly increase mean youth criminal behavior scores, by an estimated 0.16 points for each 1 point increase in the violent socialization in the community scale ($\gamma_{01}=0.156$, $p<0.001$) on average, net of violent familial socialization and gender. Higher levels of violent familial socialization also tend to significantly increase mean youth criminal behavior scores, by an estimated 0.25 points for each 1-point increase in the violent familial socialization scale ($\gamma_{10}=0.246$, $p<0.001$) on average, net of violent socialization in the community and gender. This effect is stronger for males than females, with the mean youth criminal behavior score increasing by an estimated 0.65 points for males ($\gamma_{50} = 0.645$, $p<0.001$). The predicted mean youth criminal behavior score for the prototypical male respondent who experienced violent socialization both in the community and family is approximately 6.5 points ($\gamma_{00}+\gamma_{01}+\gamma_{10}+\gamma_{50}$), on average.

Partitioning of the variance components, Model 5 shows that approximately 23% of the variation in youth criminal behavior within the same nation ($\text{Pseudo-}R^2=22.8$) can be explained by both the violent socialization and social control variables. These same variables explain about 63% of the variation in youth criminal behavior between different nations ($\text{Pseudo-}R^2=62.6$). The substantive higher explanatory power between different nations may be due to gender socialization. Gender socialization is the reinforcement of stereotypes based on cultural values of assigned gender behavior (Kendall, 2010). Such gender-based socialization seems to be a more robust predictor of criminal behavior when youth are exposed to family violence (Smagur, Bogat, & Leveondosky, 2017). Cultural-based standards reinforce certain behaviors for males but not females. As a component of gender socialization, differences in socialization experiences between males and females may include criminal behavior as a reproduction of power within society. This power is portrayed as violence in a normative response towards conflict within a nation, and this response may be exasperated for males in some nations (Delaney, 2021a). This includes violent socialization. Male youth who experienced family violence tend to have a gender-specific response to conflict (Kahn & Paluzzi, 2006; Mattingly & Straus, 2008). Violent socialization occurs within the context of a normative national-level process, both in the community and within individual families. Under such conditions, male youth who experience violent socialization would engage in more criminal behavior compared to females. This finding lends additional support to the norms of violence thesis. Youth who experience violent socialization processes engage in more criminal behavior. When pro-violent cultural contexts of nations spill over into communities and families, socialization of youth becomes impacted. Model 6 shows violent socialization within individual families continued to be variable ($T_{11} = 0.002$, $p < .05$) and this effect varies in nations with different mean youth criminal behavior scores ($T_{01} = 0.011$, $p < .01$). Such an effect may be more prominent for males, particularly when the context of violence is a normative standard for resolving conflict. The experiences with violent socialization lend for more criminal behavior among male youth (compared to female youth).

However, the null hypothesis is rejected by the intercept variance ($T_{00} = 0.080$, $p < .001$). While Model 6 provides on-going support for the norms of violence thesis, there is still some additional "explainable" variation that accounts for youth criminal behavior. And, the estimated youth criminal behavior scores within nations continue to significantly vary ($\sigma^2 = 3.078$, $p < .001$) and differences in youth criminal behavior scores across different nations continue to be significant ($T_{00} = 0.080$, $p < .001$) after controlling for violent socialization and gender. Therefore, the analysis continues with other constructs in the culture of violence theories.

Age. Age has been claimed to be a strong predictor for criminal behavior (Sweeten, Piquero, & Steinberg, 2013) including in many criminological theories. Age was included in Model 7 with gender to account for culture of violence theories contending that adolescent males engage in criminal behavior more than females. Model 7 shows that adding age to Model 6 provides no substantive change over Model 6.

Socioeconomic status. Model 8 continues to show that when youth are exposed to violent socialization processes in their families and communities ($\gamma_{10+}\gamma_{01}$), these ineffective socialization processes increase youth criminal behavior. And, the increases are more profound with increases in youths' socioeconomic status (γ_{70}). With each one-unit increase in the violent socialization in the community scale mean youth criminal behavior scores increase by an estimated 0.20 points ($\gamma_{10} = 0.201$, $p < 0.001$), on average, net of violent familial socialization and socioeconomic status. With each one-unit increase in the violent familial socialization scale mean youth criminal behavior scores increase by an estimated 0.25 points ($\gamma_{01}=0.250$, $p<0.001$), on average, net of violent socialization in the community and socioeconomic status. And, when controlling for violent socialization processes, each one-unit increase in the socioeconomic scale increases mean youth criminal behavior scores by an estimated 0.14 points ($\gamma_{70}=0.144$, $p<0.01$), on average. This is overall *less* criminal behavior compared to youth who experienced even only one type of violent socialization. The predicted youth criminal behavior score for the prototypical respondent with average socioeconomic status who experienced violent socialization is approximately 6.2 points ($\gamma_{00}+\gamma_{01}+\gamma_{10}+\gamma_{70}$), on average. Again, the normalcy of violence may be so infiltrated within nations that the collective conscious does not recognize certain behaviors and interactions as violence. And this transcends all strata within society, including socioeconomic class. In this instance, it is the more privileged youth engaging in more criminal behavior compared to the less advantaged youth.

These results offer continued support for the hypotheses, while rejecting culture of violence claims. Violent socialization, in both the micro and macro manifestations, is significantly associated with more youth criminal behavior. Violent socialization within individual families continues to be variable ($T_{11}=0.002$, $p < .01$) and this effect varies in nations with different mean youth criminal behavior scores ($T_{01} = 0.013$, $p < .05$). As socioeconomic status increases, youth criminal behavior increases. The culture of violence theories claim the opposite: youth with lower socioeconomic status engage in more criminal behavior. These results render the violence of culture theories based on socioeconomic status, moot.

The partitioning of the variance components in Model 8 shows that approximately 31% of the variation in youth criminal behavior within the same nation (Pseudo-$R^2=31.2$) can be explained by both the violent socialization and socioeconomic status. These same variables explain about 57.5% of the variation in youth criminal behavior between different nations (Pseudo- $R^2=57.5$). This model shows less explanatory power over Model 6, but still significantly improves in explanatory power over the preliminary models (Models 1–3). But, the estimated youth criminal behavior scores within nations continue to significantly vary ($\sigma^2=3.138$, $p < .001$) as a function of violent socialization processes and differences in youth criminal behavior scores across different nations continue to be significant ($T_{00}=0.091$, $p<.001$) after controlling for violent socialization and socioeconomic status. And the null hypothesis continues to be rejected (T_{00}). This may be because the model did not include all the constructs consistent with the culture of violence theories. The next model in the taxonomy includes all three main constructs of culture of violence theories.

CULTURAL FACTORS

When examining the effects of both violent socialization and all violence of culture theories (Model 9), the partition of the variance components shows approximately 23% of the variation in youth criminal behavior within the same nation (Pseudo-$R^2 = 23.11$) can be explained. In addition, about 64% of the variation in youth criminal behavior between different nations (Pseudo-$R^2 = 63.6$) can be explained. The totality of culture of violence factors offer less explanatory power within each nation, but more explanatory power between the different nations over Model 8. This seems to be in alignment with norms of violence theories. Much of culture occurs at a structural level, and that structure-based culture spills over into the micro-level institutions. Hence, more constructs that represent culture within a nation would be variant transnationally as opposed to within the same nation. And violent socialization continues to increase youth criminal behavior.

Each one-unit increase in the violent socialization within the community scale tends to increase mean youth criminal behavior scores by about 0.16 points ($\gamma_{10} = 0.160$, $p < 0.001$) net of violent familial socialization and cultural factors. With each one-unit increase in the violent familial socialization scale mean youth criminal behavior scores increase by an estimated 0.25 points ($\gamma_{01} = 0.250$, $p < 0.001$), on average, net of violent socialization in the community and cultural factors. Gender and socioeconomic status continue to be significantly associated with youth criminal behavior scores, with males ($\gamma_{50} = 0.622$, $p < 0.001$) and youth from higher socioeconomic status ($\gamma_{70} = 0.126$, $p < 0.001$) tending to engage in more criminal behavior. The predicted criminal behavior score for the prototypical male respondent, with average socioeconomic status, who experienced violent socialization is approximately 6.6 points ($\gamma_{00} + \gamma_{01} + \gamma_{10} + \gamma_{50} + \gamma_{70}$), on average.[2] In this model, the culture of a nation may be so accepting of violence that violent responses are a norm and the collective conscious no longer recognize the occurrence of certain behaviors as violence. Certainly, violence is not deviant in these nations. Instead, violence may be inured. The cultural standard spills over into socialization processes. And, in order to ensure conformity with the cultural standards, those with higher status in society may embrace norms of violence more so than those members of society with a lower status. In fact, members of society may not even recognize certain behaviors and interactions as violence. However, the null hypothesis is rejected by the intercept variance (T_{00}) in Model 9. The relationship between the violent socialization variables and youth criminal behavior could be spurious. Therefore, additional analysis is needed with all variables included in a single model.

Violent Socialization and Current Life Circumstances

Model 10 displays the results of combining all level-1 variables with violent socialization. Social desirability was included as a control in this model as a control. The results show the effects of violent socialization on youth criminal behavior remain constant: violent socialization continues to be significantly associated with increases in youth criminal behavior scores even when controlling for other theoretical constructs, both in the community (γ_{01}) and within families (γ_{10}). For each 1 point increase in the violent socialization in the community scale, mean youth criminal behavior scores tend to significantly increase, by an estimated 0.11 points for each 1 increase in the violent socialization in the community scale ($\gamma_{01}=0.113$, $p<0.001$) on average, net of violent familial socialization and other controls. For each 1 point increase in the violent familial socialization scale, mean youth criminal behavior scores tend to significantly increase, by an estimated 0.11 points ($\gamma_{10}=0.153$, $p<0.001$) on average, net of violent socialization in the community and other controls. The predicted mean youth criminal behavior score for the prototypical male respondent of average age experiencing violent socialization, but has average levels of attachments, self-control, socioeconomic status, and socially desirable responses whose peers engage in criminal behavior, is approximately 6.1 points on average.[3]

These results offer further support for the first and second hypotheses. In the nations where violent socialization processes are used, both in the community and within the family, youth in that nation tend to engage in more criminal behavior (H_1 and H_2). This finding holds true even in the presence of effective social control markers. This finding holds true regardless of other theoretical premises used to explain youth criminal behavior. Violent socialization may just be part of the life circumstances for some youth. This contention is further supported by the finding that youth criminal behavior is variable. Estimated youth criminal behavior scores within nations continue to significantly vary ($\sigma^2=2.763$, $p < .001$) and differences in youth criminal behavior scores across different nations continue to be significant ($T_{00}=0.106$, $p<.001$, net controls. The results also offer continued support for the third hypothesis. Youth criminal behavior significantly varies from nation to nation as a function of violent familial socialization processes ($T_{01}= 0.013$, $p < .01$). But Model 10 does not fully embrace the norms of violence thesis. Families are nested within nations. Some nations have structural norms supporting violence. These structural norms must be accounting in assessing the norms of violence thesis. The intercept variance (T_{00}) rejecting the null hypothesis indicates there is still additional "explainable" variation to account for youth criminal behavior.

Violent Socialization Transnationally

Examining national-level averages does not provide nation specific-information to examine the details of variation. The analysis needs to include each individual nation. In order to determine if violent socialization processes predict criminal behavior for respondents within each nation, separate regression models were run for each nation using OLS regression. By separating respondents by nation, the results can be compared to show the specific differences, across nations, in the relationship between violent socialization processes and respondents' individual criminal behavior.

The results of the OLS regression are shown in Table 5.4. By separating respondents by nation, the results show the relationship between violent

Table 5.4 Criminal Behavior Regressed on Violent Socialization, Attachment, and Self-Control for Each Nation in the IDVS

	USA (n = 4236)	*MEX (n = 235)*	*NTL (n = 410)*	*_ENG (n = 218)_*	*CHN (n = 2502)*	*ISR (n = 153)*	*SWZ (n = 161)*	*CND (n = 1199)*	*BRZ (n = 275)*
violent comm	0.145***	0.028	0.104*	0.194**	0.054	0.025	0.021	0.200***	0.006
violent family	0.134***	0.154**	0.116**	0.028	0.272***	0.275***	0.282***	0.237***	0.223**
attachment	−0.116***	−0.059	−0.162**	−0.033	−0.070**	0.069	−0.134*	0.051~	−0.076
self-control	−0.218***	−0.121***	−0.151**	−0.151*	−0.195***	−0.138**	−0.122~	−0.212***	−0.188**
peers	0.150**	−0.187	−0.194~	0.463*	0.037	−0.077	0.277	0.032	0.044
gender	0. 630***	1.165***	0.402~	0.200	0.730***	0.877**	0.781**	0.258~	0.094
age	0.017	−0.036**	−0.044	0.051	0.012	0.125	0.082	−0.024	0.079~
ses	0.128***	0.238~	0.049	0.029	0.196***	−0.053***	0.355**	0.099~	0.019
socdes	−0.040***	−0.034	−0.032~	−0.104**	−0.012	−0.011	−0.052~	−0.021	−0.042
Constant	10.213***	8.125***	9.007***	9.396***	7.343**	2.247	6.871**	8.925***	7.862***
R^2	0.385***	0.410***	0.286***	0.267***	0.312***	0.339***	0.439***	0.352***	0.348***
Adj- R^2	0.383***	0.382***	0.266***	0.231***	0.307***	0.291***	0.400***	0.346***	0.321***

*** $p < 0.001$ ** $p < 0.01$ * $p < 0.05$ ~ $p < 0.10$

(Continued)

Table 5.4 (continued)

	PGL (n=424)	*AST (n=210)*	*SKR (n=243)*	*_SNG (n=231)_*	*NZL (n=137)*	*IND (n=190)*	*BEL (n=574)*	*SCT (n=213)*	*GER (n=471)*
violent comm	0.045	0.296**	0.103	0.238**	0.159	0.052	0.164***	0.184*	0.025
violent family	0.170***	0.122*	0.248***	0.163**	0.200**	0.061	0.154***	0.176**	0.146***
attachment	−0.112**	−0.132*	−0.222**	0.129*	0.069	−0.358**	−0.093*	−0.075	−0.112**
self-control	−0.043	−0. 122*	−0.090	−0.052	−0.208*	−0.370**	−0.123***	−0.194**	−0.177***
peers	0.211	0.054	−0.363	0	0.418	−0.233	0.201	0.136	0.109
gender	0.599***	0.050	0.876**	0.454	1.327**	0.591	0.371*	0.578~	0.443*
age	0.117**	0.042	−0.056	−0.046	0.048	0.005	0.029	0.037	0.042
ses	0.225**	0.066	0.065	0.158	0.380*	0.729*	0.182**	0.329*	0.045
socdes	−0.082**	−0.071*	−0.014	−0.073~	−0.165**	−0.180**	−0.069***	−0.041	−0.089
Constant	6.164***	8.310***	9.118***	8.424***	11.320***	21.184***	8.218***	7.816***	10.972***
R^2	0.311***	0.352***	0.341***	0.352***	0.363***	0.457***	0.325***	0.347***	0.280***
Adj- R^2	0.293***	0.330***	0.306***	0.319***	0.310***	0.398***	0.313***	0.316***	0.265***

*** $p<0.001$ ** $p<0.01$ * $p<0.05$ ~ $p<0.10$

Table 5.4. (continued)

	LTH (n=448)	*IRN(n=99)*	*RSS (n=450)*	*_GRC (n=286)_*	*SWD (n=433)*	*ROM (n=271)*	*GTM (n=249)*	*HUN (n=176)*	*TWN (n=258)*
violent comm	0.064	0.023**	0.077	0.006	0.287***	0.042	0.121	0.123~	0.002
violent family	0.137***	0.109	0.182***	0.237***	0.194***	0.111**	0.131~	0.208**	0.206**
Attachment	−0.155***	−0.101	−0.190***	0.041	−0.03	−0.232***	−0.179~	0.114~	−0.059
self-control	−0.148***	−0.162~	−0.100*	−0.171**	−0.114*	−0.115**	−0.206**	−0.055	−0.220**
peers	0.149	−0.073	−0.139	0.556*	−0.038	−0.160	0.220	0.044	0.211
gender	0.705***	1.181**	0.415*	0.589*	0.675**	0.824**	0.713~	0.080	0.198
age	−0.049	−1.186	0.117**	−0.032	0.049	0.033	0	0.075	0.127
ses	0.071**	−0.026	0.350***	0.185~	0.060*	0.069*	0.103	0.202~	0.053
socdes	−0.009	−0.072	−0.114***	−0.055~	−0.064*	−0.024	−0.073	−0.033	0
Constant	9.749***	36.693	8.898***	8.706***	5.941***	8.735***	12.382***	4.647~	6.218*
R^2	0.290***	0.331***	0.365***	0.334***	0.345***	0.267***	0.312***	0.272***	0.203***
Adj- R^2	0.273***	0.263***	0.351***	0.306***	0.332***	0.239 ***	0.274***	0.227***	0.156***

*** $p<0.001$ ** $p<0.01$ * $p<0.05$ ~ $p<0.10$

(Continued)

Table 5.4. (continued)

	JPN (n = 207)	*MLT(n = 112)*	*TNZ (n = 208)*	*SAF (n = 124)_*	*VNZ (n = 249)*
violent comm	0.131	0.051	0.004	0.109	0.083
violent family	0.175**	0.205*	0.105	0.101	0.044
attachment	−0.060	−0.043	−0.151	−0.316*	−0.142*
self-control	−0.122~	−0.041	0.208*	−0.157	−0.251***
peers	0.314	0.225	0.032	0.623	−0.223
gender	0.705*	0.233	0.255	−0.534	−0.100
age	0.131	0.035	−0.025	−0.200**	0.031
Ses	−0.247~	0.251	−0.010	−0.192	0.290
socdes	0.039	−0.002	−0.133*	0.138*	0.011*
Constant	1.918	3.975	15.690***	20.330***	10.578***
R^2	0.257***	0.190*	0.266***	0.370***	0.243***
Adj- R^2	0.202***	0.100*	0.217***	0.299***	0.211***

*** $p < 0.001$ ** $p < 0.01$ * $p < 0.05$ ~ $p < 0.10$

socialization processes and respondents' individual criminal behavior varies transnationally. There are respondents in some of the nations in which their criminal behavior as a youth is not significantly associated with violent socialization processes, either in the community or within their individual family. These nations include Guatemala (GTM), India (IND), South Africa (SAF), Tanzania (TAN), and Venezuela (VZA). For the other nations, respondents' experiences with violent socialization processes significantly predict youth criminal behavior.

There was only one nation in which only community-based violent socialization processes are significantly associated with youth's criminal behavior: England (ENG).[4] Looking at England, increases in violent community socialization are significantly associated with increases in individual criminal behavior scores. With each one-unit increase in violent community socialization, youth criminal behavior scores increase by about 0.19 points ($b_1 = 0.194$, $p < 0.001$). These increases occur even in the presence of the protective factor of self-control $b_4 = -0.151$, $p < 0.05$).[5] Violent socialization within the communities in England significantly explains about 27% of the variance in youth criminal behavior ($R^2 = 0.267$, $p < 0.001$), net of controls. The predicted youth criminal behavior score for the prototypical respondent who experienced violent community socialization is approximately 9.57 points ($b_1 + b_4 +$ constant). This is about 4 points higher than the mean youth criminal score across all nations. So, the respondents who experienced violent community socialization tended to report more criminal behavior compared to respondents who did not experience violent community socialization processes.

In the majority of nations, violent familial socialization alone was significantly associated with youth's criminal behavior. The results show that respondents who experienced more violent familial socialization processes tended to report having significantly more involvement in criminal behavior prior to age 15. These countries include Brazil (BRZ), China (CHN), Germany (GER), Greece (GRC), Israel (ISR), Lithuania (LTH), Mexico (MEX), New Zealand (NZL), Portugal (PGL), Romania (ROM), Russia (RSS), S. Korea (SKR), Switzerland (SWZ), and Taiwan (TWN).[6] For example, respondents in New Zealand (NZL) who experienced violent familial socialization processes tended to have the highest predicted youth criminal behavior scores, net of controls, at 11.11 compared to youth in other nations ($b_1 + b_2 + b_4 +$ constant). This score is more than double the mean youth criminal score across all nations (see Table 4.3 for descriptive statistics). In New Zealand, self-control offered a slightly protective effect on youth criminal behavior ($b_4 = -0.208$, $p < 0.05$) whereas attachments within the family had no statistically significant effect. The lowest youth criminal behaviors scores among those who experienced violent familial socialization are in Portugal. The predicted youth criminal behavior score was only slightly above the mean, at about 6.3 points, net of controls ($b_2 + b_3 + b_4 +$ constant). In New Zealand, attachments within the family had a slight protective effect on youth criminal behavior in Portugal ($b_3 = -0.112$, $p < 0.01$) whereas self-control has no statistically significant effect.

There were several nations in which *both* violent socialization within the community and violent familial socialization were significantly associated with youth criminal behavior. These nations are Australia (AST), Belgium (BEL), Canada (CND), The Netherlands (NTL), Scotland (SCT), Singapore (SNG), Sweden (SWD), and the United States (USA). Again, comparing the highest levels of youth criminal behavior to the lowest levels, respondents in the United States who experienced violent socialization processes tended to have the highest predicted youth criminal behavior scores, net of controls, with a prototypical score of 10.16 compared to youth in other nations ($b_1+b_2+b_3+b_4+$ constant). This is taking into account the protective factors of attachments ($b_3=-0.116$, $p<0.001$) and self-control ($b_4=-0.218$, $p<0.001$), which were both significantly associated with less youth criminal behavior. This score is still more than double the mean youth criminal score across all nations (see Table 4.3 for descriptive statistics). The lowest youth criminal behavior scores among those who experienced violent socialization are in Sweden. The predicted youth criminal behavior score was only slightly above the mean, at about 6.3 points, net of controls ($b_1+b_2+b_3+b_4+$ constant). This includes the protective factor of self-control ($b_4=-0.114$, $p<0.001$).[7]

These results continue to provide support for the norms of violence thesis. To some degree, violent socialization processes are associated with youth criminal behavior across most nations. The effect of violent socialization on youth criminal behavior varies from nation to nation.

In 22 nations, respondents' experiences with violent socialization processes were significantly associated with their criminal behavior as youth. Further analyses were conducted to look for specific patterns: group analysis by region.

Using the regional categorizations from the IDVS (see http://pubpages.unh.edu/~mas2/Nations1.htm), the results seem to reflect similarities by region with few exceptions. In the African nations, violent socialization processes were not significantly associated with respondents' criminal behavior during youth. In the Asian nations, violent socialization processes were significantly associated with respondents' criminal behavior in all nations but Japan and India. In all the European nations, violent socialization processes were significantly associated with respondents' criminal behavior during youth.[8] In both Australia and New Zealand, violent socialization processes were significantly associated with respondents' criminal behavior during youth. This is also true for the North American nations. It is only the Latin American nations that produced strong mixed results: in half the nations, violent socialization processes were significantly associated with respondents' criminal behavior during youth. It is worth noting that in the Middle Eastern nations (i.e., Iran and Israel), the overall regression models were not statistically significant and therefore cannot be included in this OLS regression analysis. Unfortunately, there tend to be disparities between the Middle Eastern nations and the other nations in the IDVS. For example, the two Middle Eastern nations (Iran and Israel) have a religion-specific context to the nation's structure. Thus, further research is necessary to discover what societal influences may be present in the Middle Eastern nations to explain youth criminal behavior.

These geographical-regional results partially support the first and second hypothesis: *youth from families that use violent socialization processes will engage in more criminal behavior, compared to youth from families that use non-violent familial socialization processes, even in the presence of effective familial socialization processes* (H_1), and *youth in communities that use violent socialization processes will engage in more criminal behavior, compared to youth in communities that do not use violent socialization processes* (H_2). This analysis was useful to support the need for multilevel modeling regression analysis. Multilevel modeling regression analysis can determine if there are significant variations in youth criminal behavior scores across different nations and if violent socialization processes could account for this variation.

Nation Structure as Part of Norms of Violence

To begin the examination of the structural context of norms of violence, the structural indicators of violence are compared. As discussed in previous chapters, these are the formal conditions within a nation that either promote a culture of pro-violence or abdicate violence. The conditions include aggregate levels of violent socialization, laws prohibiting the use of corporal punishment on children, laws abolishing the death penalty, and homicide rates. The conditions are indicators of violence, a context in which violence is either more normalized or not. While these conditions may seem limited, as discussed in the Methodology section, transnational measures are challenging due to the lack of comparable definitions and consistency in measurement for such variables.

The Context of Life Circumstances

Table 5.5 lists indicators of violence, by nation. There appears to be variation in the scores for each of these indicators of violence across the different nations. However, by focusing the analysis on nations with higher scores and lower scores among these various indicators of violence, there are some patterns. Some nations hold consistently high scores across the indicators of violence. But there are also some nations with low scores on the indicators of crime.

An example of a nation with higher scores on the indicators of violence is Mexico. This nation has an overall higher mean violent socialization score (16.32) compared to other nations' mean violent socialization scores. Mexico has no laws prohibiting the use of physical discipline against youth (no). And although Mexico does not formally use the death penalty (no), there is a high homicide rate (13.24) compared to other nations. Brazil reflects similar statistics:

higher mean violent socialization score (13.99), no laws prohibiting the use of physical discipline against youth (no), and a high homicide rate (33.80). The difference in these nations is that Brazil supports the use of the death penalty

Table 5.5 Indicators of Violence, By Nation (IDVS)

Country	*Mean violent socialization*	*Anti-physical discipline law*	*Use of death penalty*	*Mean homicide rate*[a]
Australia	13.80	No	No	1.57
Belgium	11.93	Yes	No	2.10
Brazil	13.99	No	Yes	33.80
Canada	13.88	Yes	No	1.92
China	15.74	Yes	Yes	2.47
England	14.32	Yes	No	1.53
Germany	14.35	Yes	No	1.23
Greece	14.54	Yes	No	1.32
Guatemala	14.81	Yes	Yes	33.68
Hungary	13.41	Yes	No	2.32
India	14.88	No	Yes	4.01
Iran	13.87	Yes	Yes	--
Israel	13.26	Yes	Yes	2.72
Japan	13.52	Yes	Yes	0.5
Lithuania	14.25	Yes	No	--
Malta	13.69	Yes	No	0.95
Mexico	16.32	No	No	13.24
Netherlands	12.60	Yes	No	1.32
New Zealand	13.53	Yes	No	1.34
Portugal	14.22	Yes	No	1.10
Romania	14.25	Yes	No	2.68
Russia	15.22	Yes	Yes	--
Scotland	15.81	Yes	No	2.25
Singapore	13.55	No	Yes	0.81
S. Africa	16.73	Yes	No	49.56
S. Korea	16.16	No	Yes[b]	2.18
Sweden	11.88	Yes	No	1.03
Switzerland	13.62	Yes	No	1.10
Taiwan	17.22	Yes	Yes	5.68
Tanzania	17.12	No	Yes	--
United States	14.85	No	Yes	6.09
Venezuela	14.38	Yes	No	31.00

[a] Nations with—had less than 10 years of data for the homicide rate: Brazil (3 years), China (4 years), Malta (6 years), South Korea (6 years). Nations marked with—had no data available for homicide rates.

[b] Poland and South Korea retain laws that support the use of death penalty.

(yes). These countries, among others, appear to hold structures in which violence is a more accepted use of social control, creating a context in which youth criminal behavior would also be expected to be higher (compared to other nations). These countries could be nations in which violence is a normative standard, and this "norm" spills over into other domains of society. The norms supporting violence are reproduced within socialization processes.

Sweden is a nation with low scores across the indicators of violence. Within Sweden, the overall mean violent socialization score (11.88) is low compared to other nations' mean violent socialization scores. Sweden has laws that prohibit the use of physical discipline against youth (yes) and does not use the death penalty as a form of criminal sanction (no). The mean national homicide rate is also low (1.03) in relation to the mean homicide rate for other nations. It would appear, overall, that there may be less violence in Sweden. Belgium is another example, and the statistics mirror Sweden: lower mean violent socialization score (11.93), laws prohibiting the use of physical discipline against youth (yes), not using of the death penalty (no), and a low homicide rate (2.10). The norms within these northern European nations may influence socialization such that violence, in any form, may be considered an unacceptable method of social control.

The analysis of indicators of violence across different nations preliminarily offers a general sense of violence occurring within a context specific to any given nation. By separating data by nation, the results can be compared to show the specific differences within each nation and make a superficial comparison across nations through OLS regression. Yet, there may be a contextual effect in which criminal behavior varies as a function of violent socialization processes. But as discussed previously in this book, OLS regression analysis is not sufficient for analyzing such a contextual effect (Hamilton, 2013). In order to determine if a contextual effect does exist within these 32 nations, the complete data need to be explored using multilevel modeling regression analysis in order to examine the degree to which criminal behavior varies across different nations as a function of violent socialization processes. MLM regression analysis needs to confirm the presence of a contextual effect while controlling for these structural indicators of violence. Therefore, the analyses continue with MLM regression, examining whether or not violent socialization processes, as part of norms of violence within any given nation, are significantly associated with youth criminal behavior. The analysis includes the extent to which variance in youth criminal behavior can be explained by violent socialization processes. This analysis is expected to lend support to the norms of violence thesis, by demonstrating that the structurally supported culture of violence theoretically spills over into multiple dimensions of life circumstances and renders social control ineffective. Multiple dimensions of violence are interrelated in such a way that a context is created within nations that either reinforce or reject violence.

Violent Socialization within a Context

Returning to Table 5.3, Model 11 adds the contextual indicators of violence (additional level-2 variables) to the taxonomy of multi-models. The effects of both manifestations of violent socialization combined with the measures of violence within nations, all other theoretical indicators, and controls on youth criminal behavior are statistically significant. The partitioning of the variance components shows approximately 30.5% of the variation in youth criminal behavior within the same nation (Pseudo-$R^2 = 30.5$) can be explained. In

addition, about 42% of the variation in youth criminal behavior between different nations (Pseudo-$R^2 = 42.1$) can be explained by these same variables. This combination of factors offers about the same explanatory power within each nation, but the explanatory power between the different nations is reduced from Model 10. But there is still more explanatory power between nations than within nations. This seems to be in alignment with norms of violence theories. Much of culture occurs at a structural level, and that structure-based culture spills over into the micro-level institutions. Hence, more constructs that represent culture within a nation would be less variant intra-nationally compared to transnationally.

Violent socialization continues to increase youth criminal behavior. Each one-unit increase in the violent socialization within the community scale tends to increase mean youth criminal behavior scores by about 0.11 points ($\gamma_{10} = 0.112$, $p < 0.001$) net of violent familial socialization and cultural factors. With each one-unit increase in the violent familial socialization scale, mean youth criminal behavior scores increase by an estimated 0.15 points ($\gamma_{01} = 0.150$, $p < 0.001$), on average, net of violent socialization in the community and cultural factors. Two of the cultural indicators of violence also increase youth criminal behavior. For the nations where death penalty is used, mean youth criminal behavior scores tend to increase by about 0.38 points ($\gamma_{03} = 0.376$, $p < 0.01$) net of both violent socialization and controls. Each one-unit increase in homicide rate tends to increase mean youth criminal behavior scores by about 0.01 points ($\gamma_{03} = 0.012$, $p < 0.05$) net of violent socialization and controls. There was no statistically significant association between nations with laws prohibiting the use of corporal punishment on children and youth criminal behavior. The predicted criminal behavior score for the prototypical average aged male respondent of average socioeconomic status with high self-control who experienced violent socialization, but came from families with strong attachments, in nations in which the structure supports violence and friends engage in criminal behavior is approximately 6.3 points, on average.[9]

This model yields a higher youth criminal behavior score over Model 10. Thus, the addition of cultural indicators to violent socialization contributes to youth criminal behavior. Cultural structure of a nation spills over into the everyday life of its members. When this structure includes violence, this spillover includes socialization processes. The consequence is norms of violence, and these norms of violence are associated with youth criminal behavior. These results offer further support for the first and second hypotheses. In the nations for which violent socialization processes are used, both in the community and within the family, youth in that nation tend to engage in more criminal behavior (H_1). This finding holds true even in the presence of effective social control markers (H_2) and other theoretical premises used to explain youth criminal behavior. With the contextual indicators, youth criminal behavior increases more. This is the way of life in some nations: violence is the norm.

But these norms of violence vary nation to nation. Youth criminal behavior is variable, such that the estimated scores within nations continue to significantly vary ($\sigma^2 = 2.769$, $p < .001$) and the differences in youth criminal behavior scores across different nations continue to be significant ($T_{00} = 0.124$, $p < .001$), net controls. The results offer continued support for the third hypothesis. Youth criminal behavior significantly varies nation to nation as a function of violent familial socialization processes ($T_{01} = 0.013$, $p < .01$). Model 10 appears to fully embrace the norms of violence thesis. This supports the third hypothesis: youth criminal behavior significantly varies nation to nation as a function of violent socialization processes, and this serves within a context of norms of violence. The structural norms within some nations support violence, and spill over into the functions of everyday life. This spillover effect impacts socialization processes in such a way that the methods of social control used to prevent youth criminal behavior are ineffective. Instead, violent socialization processes contribute to an increase in youth's inclination towards criminal behavior. Violence is then reinforced as part of the normative cultural structure of a nation. But with the intercept variance (T_{00}) rejecting the null hypothesis, there is still additional "explainable" variation to account for youth criminal behavior and additional analysis is needed.

Continuing with the contextual analysis, Model 12 (Table 5.3), this final model includes all level-1 and level-2 predictor variables along with all control variables. Even with the addition of a level-2 control variable, Gross Domestic Product (*GDP*), the effect of violent socialization continues to significantly increase youth criminal behavior. *GDP* has no significant effect within the model. The predicted criminal behavior score for the prototypical respondent does not substantively change over Model 11: approximately 6.4 points on the youth criminal behavior scale.[10] What does change in this model is an increase in the partitioning of the variance internationally: Model 12 explains that there is an increase of about 12% in the variation in youth criminal behavior between different nations (Pseudo-$R^2 = 47.2$) that can be explained by violent socialization, net controls, over Model 11. There is no change in the intranational explanatory power over Model 11. This analysis could continue indefinitely with infinite variables. After 12 models revealing consistent effects of violent socialization on youth criminal behavior, particularly in the presence of cultural indicators of violence, the MLM analysis demonstrates sufficient support for norms of violence thesis.

Violent Norms and Youth Criminal Behavior

Overall, the results of these analyses show that, on average, youth criminal behavior is significantly increased by violent socialization processes. This is not just an individual effect of family to youth processes, but aggregate levels of youth criminal behavior vary as a function of violent socialization across nations. The analyses also indicate that youth criminal behavior is best explained through a combination of violent socialization processes and the national context in which these socialization processes occur. This context involves the structure and life circumstances within certain nations normalizing violence as a method of social control more so than other nations. Specifically, a cultural norm accepting violence is more prevalent within some nations and positively contributes to youth criminal behavior.

The results show, overall, very low youth criminal behavior scores. While youth criminal behavior scores ranged from 4 points to 16 points, the mean youth criminal behavior score for all respondents was approximately 6 points. This may be relative to these youths' status as college students. Criminal behavior should be low amongst college students because, according to self-control theory, those with low self-control would lack the self-discipline and foresight necessary to successfully attain college-level status (*cf.* Gottfresdon & Hirschi, 1990). More importantly, the results indicate that criminal behavior scores were lowest among those youth who reported both more attachments within their family and higher levels of self-control. It has been argued that criminological theory, in general, tends to reject the importance of the family in influencing behavior among adolescents (Schroeder, Giordano, & Cernkovich, 2010). But, certain familial socialization processes are widely supported as being associated with preventing youth's criminal behavior (Schmalleger & Bartollas, 2008). This includes attachments within the family and self-control. The results of the present study are consistent with the latter argument.

Violent Socialization as Part of a Norm of Violence

The results further show support for the hypotheses presented in Chapter 3. Violent socialization, overall, is associated with increased youth criminal behavior. Even when controlling for other theoretical explanations for youth criminal behavior, this relationship remains constant. There is support for the norms of violence thesis: when youth are exposed to violent socialization processes in their families and communities, these ineffective socialization processes increase youth criminal behavior. Violence may be normalized and accepted more so if youth experience only one type of violent socialization. For example, while the family may normalize the use of violence as a means to control youth behavior, youth are exposed to communities within their nation that do not practice violent socialization processes and this decreases youth criminal behavior (both individually and averages among the aggregate). This may communicate to youth that certain socialization practices are deviant despite the normalization of such practices within their family. As a result, these youth may be less inclined to engage in criminal behavior. However, if youth are exposed to violent socialization from both their families and within their communities, youth criminal behavior increases (both individually and averages among the aggregate).

In addition, the present study found that among nations with laws favoring violent social control over criminal offenders, i.e., use of death penalty, mean national levels of youth criminal behavior tended to increase (on average). And increases in homicide rates were associated with increases in the mean national level of youth criminal behavior (on average). These findings begin to provide information about the contextual effect contributing to norms of violence within a nation. The structures of nations may exasperate youth criminal behavior to the extent these structures spill over into other conditions within society. This creates a national context effect. In the present study, this national context effect is violence.

Criminal Behavior across Different Nations

One of the goals of this study was to explore the extent to which violent socialization processes are associated with youth criminal behavior. Violent socialization processes were hypothesized to have a victimizing effect on youth, becoming a risk factor for criminal behavior instead of preventing youths' criminal behavior. In other words, violent socialization processes would be associated with *more* youth criminal behavior. The results of this exploratory study supported this hypothesis: violent socialization processes both within the family and from the community were associated with significantly more youth criminal behavior. These findings are not "washed out" when accounting for other prominent theoretical explanations: social control and learning theories.

Given these findings, socialization processes intended to control youth behavior may not prevent crime when violence is part of the methods parents and other adults in the community use as control. Thus, not all socialization processes work equally to control youth behavior. These findings are supported by previous studies, which found that violent socialization was associated with other types of criminal behavior (Delaney, 2015; Delaney, 2021a; Delaney, 2021b). Further, the association between socialization processes and youth criminal behavior is more complex than primary socialization within the family or even the communities in which families reside. It involves societal influence above and beyond individual families and communities.

Another goal of the present study was to explore if youth criminal behavior across nations varied as a function of violent socialization processes, within the context of national norms supporting violence. In other words, the present study examined the degree to which violent socialization processes varied across nations as part of the context in which violence is part of the norms within that nation, and if this variation was associated with differences in youth criminal behavior in those nations. The results of this exploratory study support this hypothesis: youth criminal behavior significantly varies as a function of violent socialization processes. Structural norms supporting violence are also associated with increased youth criminal behavior. Socialization processes occur through informal mechanisms in which violence has become a norm to control behavior of the members of a nation. When structural conditions support violence at the same time that aggregates across a nation to expose youth to socialization processes involving violence, the standard of violence as a means of social control becomes socially acceptable. This is norms of violence.

But the extent to which violence is part of the norms within each nation seems to vary. Violent socialization processes are unique to a nation, occurring in conjunction with other manifestations of violence. Such violence is reflected not only in the social conditions of a nation that establish formal norms (i.e., laws), but violent social conditions may also be reflected in the informal norms within a nation, such as behaviors among the citizenry. These behaviors are particularly important surrounding conflict and conflict resolution. Such behavior includes homicide rates. With the predominant motivation for homicides characterized as conflict situations (see Morrall, 2006, for a more in-depth explanation), this type of group behavior becomes another indicator of national structure existing within a context of permissible violence. Both laws and group behavior are part of socialization processes that, over periods of time, evolve into the normative experiences of the citizenry within each nation. When these socialization processes are embedded with violence, norms of violence are present. These norms are initiated by victimizing youth through violent socialization processes and then perpetuated by youth acting out through criminal behavior. The results from this study show support for these theoretical propositions.

While violent socialization has been shown to significantly vary across different nations, these statistics cannot explain why this variation occurs or the complete context in which such variation occurs. Yet there is some published research that has explored possible contextual explanations in support of the results of the present study. Among nations with laws prohibiting the use of physical discipline on children, the citizenry tends to hold less social approval for this disciplinary practice (Zolotor & Puzia, 2010). The results from the present study also do not attest to whether or not aggregates of the citizenry within some nations are more prone toward values and beliefs supporting violence. The present study focuses on behaviors, not belief systems. Further research is necessary to explore why a context of violence exists in some nations and to explain how norms of violence may occur within these nations.

The present study is one of the first to show variation in violent socialization processes across different nations predicting youth criminal behavior. Youth criminal behavior tends to be less when they are raised in families and communities that do not use or use very little violent socialization processes. Thus, even when social forces within a nation favor violent socialization processes (e.g., physical discipline) the methods of socialization used within individual families offer some degree of protection from the effects of violence within the nation. Further, the present study demonstrates the presence of a contextual effect within some nations: violent socialization processes are associated with significantly more youth criminal behavior, on average, but this association only occurs within some nations. The lack of constant findings across all nations supports the norms of violence thesis. Not all nations endorse violence, either at the structural level or within individual families and communities. The present study offers on-going support for understanding the influence of ineffective socialization processes on youth criminal behavior. The findings further present the opportunity to understand the contexts in which latent manifestations of violence within a nation fails to contribute to controlling youth criminal behavior.

Notes

1 The calculated ICC is 0.214/(3.985 + 0.214) = 0.057.
2 Age still does not offer a significant contribution to the model.
3 This score is from adding the coefficients for γ_{00} through γ_{01} in Model 10.
4 The overall regression model was not statistically significant for Iran, and therefore is not included in this analysis.
5 Attachments within the family are not statistically significant.
6 The overall regression models were not statistically significant for Hungary, Israel, Japan, or Malta, and therefore were not included in this analysis.
7 Attachments within the family have no statistically significant effect.
8 Malta and Hungary did not overall statistically significant regression models, and were not included in this analysis.
9 This score is from adding all the coefficients for γ_{00} through γ_{04} in Model 11, Table 5.3.
10 This score is from adding all the coefficients for γ_{00} through γ_{05} in Model 12, Table 10.

Chapter 6

What Do We Do

The Implications for Norms of Violence

Violence does not occur within a vacuum. Rather, violence occurs within a context for which nations create a normative pro-violent environment, through the various norms that support violent methods of social control. This environment spills over into the socialization processes used to control youth behavior. These socialization processes occur at both the macro-level (nation-wide and communities) and micro-level (individual families). This book sought to answer the question: do violent socialization processes, at both the macro- and micro-levels, truly control youth behavior? The research in this book quantitatively tested an integrated theory of social control and culture of violence to answer this question. And the answer is: no.

Intuitively, this seems an obvious answer. But in the course of answering this question, more important information arose that propels our current knowledge about criminological theories and the study of crime/victimization. First, a new integrated theory of social control and culture of violence was offered. Criminology has failed to construct universal explanations for the causes of crime across different nations (Johnson & Barak-Glantz, 1983) until now. The spillover effect of norms of violence offers a theoretical proposition to help explain youth criminal behaviors transnationally. The findings from the present study, as presented in this book, suggests that nation-based contexts of violence spill over into the socialization processes of communities and families and this spillover effect results in norms of violence within a nation. Such norms fail to offer adequate control over youth behavior. This failure is demonstrated as youth criminal behavior. One of the reasons that youth behavior is not controlled through violent socialization processes is the victimizing effects on youth. Thus, norms of violence is a theory that elucidates both victimization and youth criminal behavior. And the theory holds true even in the presence of competing theories of crime.

Second, the implications of this study on the norms of violence is research that can guide measures to be taken to prevent both victimization and youth criminal behavior. The research finds that violent socialization tends to be more prevalent among nations with indicators of normalized pro-violence compared to nations without such indicators, and these processes and indicators are associated with increased youth criminal behavior. These findings are true even in the presence of protective factors of social control. Violent socialization processes, supported by structural norms of violent social control within a nation, can be considered child abuse. Child abuse is a public health concern (Jung, Herrenkohl, Lee, Hemphill, Heerde, & Skinner, 2017).

This leads to the most important implication of norms of violence: the victimizing effect of violent socialization. As discussed in previous chapters, exposure to violence is a victimizing experience. Youth who are victimized through violence, particularly socialized through a range of normative violence during their developmental years, may inculcate violent behavior as acceptable conflict resolution. Violence-based experiences can translate into normative behavioral responses (Gorman-Smith & Tolan, 1998). And, youth can experience trauma and subsequent mental health issues as a result of violent victimization experiences (Kennedy, Edmonds, Dann, & Burnett, 2010; Kerig, 2019; Negriff, 2020; Widom & Maxfield, 2001). The combination of mental health impacts and acting out behavior pose risk for youth to engage in criminal behavior. This is particularly salient when living in communities and nations that espouse violence. And this effect holds true transnationally. The victimizing effect, then, is violence victimization as a risk factor for criminal behavior across different nations despite cultural variation (see Delaney, 2021b).

Norms of Violence

Some social control theorists may argue that the fundamental motivational arguments of social control and culture-based theories cannot be aligned. Is youth behavior controlled (versus not controlled) or does the behavior originate from the cultural structure of a nation? Are these perspectives truly opposing and incompatible arguments? The norms of violence thesis argues that the two perspectives can be integrated to provide a more comprehensive understanding of the conditions that fail to contribute to the prevention of youth criminal behavior across different nations. Culture permeates all aspects of a nation, from the laws that set precedent for acceptable and unacceptable behavior to the informal norms within families that define youth behavior. Culture is comprised, in part, of the norms of a nation, and these norms are filtered through the structures of a nation. The formal and informal structures of a nation contribute to the socialization of all members within that nation. One of the major goals of socialization is the control of youth behavior. Therefore, the culture of a nation cannot be separated from any explanation of control over youth behavior, particularly the prevention of youth criminal behavior.

When nation-based norms include violence, the cultural structure of a pro-violent nation spills over into other domains of society, including socialization processes. The two theoretical positions of social control theories and culture based theories overlap and support each other. Within some nations, violence may not be considered deviant behavior. Instead, aggregates of families within the same nation may be conforming to the norms of that nation (Nurco & Lerner, 1999). Thus, families and communities engage violent socialization processes in order to conform to societal norms. The circumstances of life in some nations may be that violence is a normative experience, both through formal norms (laws) and informal norms (socialization). The findings from the present study support this. The research presented in this book supports these contentions.

These findings are particularly important because the present study is one of the first to demonstrate that Gottfredson and Hirschi's stability thesis does not hold weight across different nations, as no other international studies were located that specifically examine the effects of socialization process as a contextual effect for youth criminal behavior. Instead, variation in the use of violent socialization processes, within a larger context of normative violence within the nation, may be an important factor for explaining youth criminal behavior transnationally.

The results from the present study begin to offer evidence to support the norms of violence thesis. The research used quantitative methods exclusively. Given the limits of quantitative research for explaining such social phenomenon, the present study cannot offer the specific reasons why violent socialization processes may vary from nation to nation. Instead, the theoretical propositions presented as the norms of violence thesis in this book are, at this time, preliminary.Future research is necessary to specifically examine other social and life conditions that might also contribute to a contextual effect of violence within nations and the specific reasons violent socialization processes may vary from nation to nation. However, the present study helps to move forward violence-based research seeking to examine potential consequences of socially approved violence within socialization processes that may become part of the context in which youth are socialized.

It is time to move past the debilitating debate of which criminological theory is more important. Criminologists need to begin to examine a more nuanced theories that incorporate both social control theories, to explain the effects of ineffective socialization during children's formative years, combined with culture-based theories, to explain the spill over of structural factors into socialization processes, and how the integration of the main concepts of these theories are contributing factors to a victimizating effect on youth and ensuing criminal behavior.At the same time, criminological theories need to incorporate an exploration of this context in which both socialization and culture may prevent youth criminal behavior across different nations.

Moving Beyond Current Theories

Norms of violence extends current criminological theory. Social control theories fail to explicitly discuss variation in socialization across different nations. As such, these theories cannot account for why violent socialization processes, occurring within a context of norms of violence, would be associated with increased youth criminal behavior. As such, criminology may have to sacrifice the desire for an all-encompassing general theory of crime to produce a more comprehensive theory that recognizes the combination of the complexity of socialization processes and the influences of norms on socialization processes effecting youth criminal behavior. A comprehensive theory needs to be an integrative theory that blends the core theoretical premises of two or more major criminological theories.

One way of integrating two different criminological theories is to conceive of macro-level characteristics as influencing the attitudes, relationships, and behavior of individuals. For example, when violence is reinforced through societal norms, the effects of these norms may be associated with both group-level socialization processes (i.e., socialization processes occurring across different communities) and individual-level familial socialization processes. The norms of violence thesis, and accompanying research in this book, begin to offer this integrated approach.

In addition to being an integrated social control-culture of violence theory, the norms of violence thesis expands upon Straus' (2010) criminogenic theory: the norms of violence thesis moves beyond examining singular dimensions of violence (i.e., physical discipline) and expounds a more robust contextual effect within nations. The results of the present study show support for the contextual effects of violence weakening the ability to enact social control over youth behavior and instead exasperates youth criminal behavior.

The norms of violence thesis also expands Oetting's (1999) learning theory of primary socialization (PST). PST argues that youth behavior is learned through multiple mechanism of social, psychological, and cultural conditions through the context of agents of primary socialization (Oetting, & Donnermeyer, 2009). The family tends to be the origin of socialization processes (Kendall, 2010). Oetting, instead, focuses mostly on peer relationships occurring during adolescence and the strength of those peer relationships rather than the impact of socialization throughout the life course on youth deviant behavior. PST fails to fully account for the socialization that occurs during childhood prior to adolescence. This is an important consideration because the influence of violent socialization processes early in life may be sustaining (see e.g., Maughan & Gardner, 2010). The norms of violence thesis supports PST in that youth socialized via a process of violence may stem from the norms expressed within the family and these norms would most likely induce criminal behavior during adolescence.

However, PST focuses on deviant behavior. Not all youth criminal behavior may be considered deviant. As discussed throughout this book, violence may be considered a norm within some nations.The present study found that, in some nations, violent familial socialization processes had no effect on individual youth's criminal behavior. This may be the result of variation in individual familial behaviors. This variation could be attributed to variation in the degree to which relationships between parents and youth are positive and functional (Maughan & Gardner, 2010). For example, some families might engage only one dimension of violent socialization processes, such as violent discipline. Violent discipline may be viewed as a functional aspect of socialization processes within the community and nation in which the family resides, while the other dimensions of violent socialization processes may be considered deviant within that nation. PST fails to account for the inure effect of normative violence on youth criminal behavior. Because the present study examined a typology of violent familial socialization processes, future studies could compare the effects of each type of violent familial socialization on criminal behavior.

The norms of violence thesis extend the arguments of the criminogenic effect and PST from family and community into the cultural structure of the nation. Within socialization processes, the context of a nation's structure cannot be parsed out from the life circumstances of youth. There is an effect of the national context spilling over into socialization processes, particularly when the effect is a normative standard of violent social control. This spillover impacts both families and communities. The standards of a nation are pervasive in social exchange within society and impact all levels, from the nation as a whole to communities to families. Therefore, while the family's influence over youth behavior may wane over time in favor of more community-based influences in socialization processes, individual-level effects cannot be separated out from the context in which these effects occur. A more ecological approach in explaining the impact of socialization processes on youth criminal behavior needs to be considered. This is the norms of violence thesis.

And finally, the present study offers a theory that transverses the criminal behavior-victimization division. The study of criminology need not be a polarized approach, where researchers focus on either criminal behavior or crime victimization. As normative as violence may be, there are consequences to pro-violent social control nations. Violence creates a trauma-based society. Trauma victimizies youth and has consequences on their development. One consequence is crime. This victimization-crime paradox is simply an intricate web of experiences at varying levels and domains within society that compound into life circumstances. The field of criminology needs to continue moving forward in exploring the complexities of these life circumstances.

Violent Socialization Processes

One of these life experiences is socialization processes. As found in this book and the research cited in this book, violence-based methods of socialization, ultimately, offer little to no control over youth's behavior. This expands the current literature, which has found that individual indicators of violent socialization processes have, independent of each other, consistently predicted criminal behavior (see Goddard, Goff, Melancon, & Huebner, 2000). Violent socialization processes vary from nation to nation and these differences across nations predict the degree to which youth engage in criminal behavior. Violent socialization processes are part of the overarching "norms of violence" in which violence is more tolerated within certain nations.

Social Control and Youth Criminal Behavior across Different Nations

The overall results of the present study should be interpreted as the need for varying approaches toward the control of youth behavior, and specifically youth criminal behavior. International crime prevention must be nation specific, given the nuances in the cultural structure of nations. Prevention techniques need to consider the unique characteristics of each nation that might contribute to overall violence. This is particularly crucial, given that preventive efforts are non-existent in many nations (Hayhurst, Sundstrom, & Arksey, 2018). Most nations have yet to determine what constitutes ineffective socialization processes, particularly surrounding the use of physical discipline (Knowles, 1996). Changes need to occur to support families and communities nested within nations so that youth criminal behavior can be prevented.

Social Control within a Culture of Violence

Social control theories make a fundamental distinction from other theories of crime: human beings are naturally prone toward criminal acts, and motivation is not relevant in the explanation of criminal behavior. Based on this fundamental assertion, the justice systems may be ineffective at crime prevention if the focus of a justice system is rational choice and deterrence. Nations that consider criminal behavior to be rational seem to take the philosophy of deterrence in enacting punishments on criminal offenders. The offenders are punished in such a way as to communicate to members of the nation that the behavior will not be tolerated. Yet this has not prevented or stopped criminal behavior. Some of these nations, such as the United States, have high violent crime rates compared to the nations in the world (Messner & Rosenfeld, 2008). This paradigm is ineffective at controlling crime. There has been little empirical support for rational choice and deterrence theories of crime (Paternoster & Pogarsky, 2009). Rather than focusing on *why* youth commit crime and assigning the punishments for criminal behavior as a means for deterrence, perhaps it is time for justice systems to focus on why youth *conform* to the law. In other words, the focus needs to be on prevention: doing what *works* to keep youth from engaging in criminal behavior.

The control aspects of the norms of violence thesis argue that current justice systems tend to be ineffective in crime prevention. Effective socialization that prevents youth criminal behavior occurs before pre-adolescence (Gottfredson & Hirschi, 1990). Since most criminal sanctions tend to aim toward youth older than about the age of 15, punishment through formal justice system channels would not effectively control crime. One important consideration is that levels of personal control *vary* throughout the life course (*cf.* Sampson, & Laub, 1993). The tenet of control theory indicates that reform to justice systems are fruitless because youth with low self-control will engage in crime regardless of the sanctions for their criminal behavior. And, the period in the life course when criminal behavior typically declines or ceases all together is the adult years (Steffensmeier & Streifel, 1991). The regulatory impact of the family then maintains cohesion for the youth, by forcing the youth into conformity. When youth feel they belong to a particular social group (e.g., family), youth experience a great sense of social integration (*c.f.* Durkheim, 1966 [1933]). This social integration serves to curb youth's desires toward criminal behavior.

What Do We Do?

Since international agencies have argued for the need to study the effects of violence (United Nations, 2006b) and there is a current criminological argument that social scientists are morally obligated to prevent risk of harm to youth (Luthar & Goldstein, 2008), the research presented in this book can serve to inform both academics and practitioners. So how do we curb these norms of violence? There are a number of resources and policy changes that can be implemented to combat norms of violence across different nations.

Familial Supports

Services need to address familial socialization processes, such that the methods of control parents exert over youth move away from violence-based techniques. Intervention programs cannot focus prevention solely on children, nor primarily benefit children. Families are responsible for their children's socialization, not the children. One means in which to offer family support is to address parental knowledge of child development. Parenting-based programs can be offered to families during and post pregnancy. Medical providers seem to strongly encourage childbirth classes to "learn" how to give birth, a process that lasts for hours. Socializing children and youth occurs over years, yet no one encourages parenting classes. This is not to say that parenting should be "licensed", but rather the focus on providing parents to be with skills, social supports, and *knowledge* about child-rearing issues (e.g. child development, effective discipline techniques). These services inform parents of the basic developmental stages for children, which would not only prepare parents for the behaviors typically encountered in children at different stages, but also provide parents with a framework for developing effective strategies to counteract deviant behavior throughout the child's life course.

As discussed throughout this book, the family is expected to regulate and control youth behavior (Bui, 2009). Once parents learn why children behave the way they do, parents can provide age-appropriate non-violent discipline

(Pople, 2010). These programs have been found to prevent adverse childhood outcomes (Olds, 2007) and prevent youth criminal behavior (Cullen, Vose, Lero Jonson, & Unnever, 2007; Petro, 2010). These parenting programs can set the foundation for familial attachments, by increasing parent-child bonds, and future self-regulated behavior among youth. One of the best crime control methods is primary intervention for parents.

These parenting programs would be ideal. Social welfare agencies may have attempted to implement similar programs, such as home-based aides. But these aides are temporary in nature, and funding issues prevent the widespread use of such aides. Social welfare programs often fail in capitalistic society: these agencies are typically non-profit and not well funded, if funded at all. Capitalism focuses on profits, not the welfare of the citizenry. Governments may not provide adequate funding, as the reliance for government funds stem from the taxes imposed on the members of the nation. Politics and the popular consensus of a nation lend the allocation of tax monies to fluctuate. Thus, parenting programs could possibly succeed if more readily available and adequately funded. But this may not be possible in some nations, particularly among the less economically advantaged nations.

The findings of this study support the need to ensure strong integration of youth within their families. The present study found that stronger attachments within the family were associated with significantly less self-reported criminal behavior. These findings are consistent with the current research. Since trust tends to be the cornerstone of family relations (Giddens, 1991), the role of attachments within the family may serve as collective efficacy (Mazerolle, Wickes, & McBroom, 2010) to strengthen control over youth behavior. But when attachments are weak in the family, youth may be more likely to engage in criminal behavior (Nurco & Lerner, 1999). Familial socialization processes may only be truly ineffective when attachments within the family are weak (*cf.* Hirchi, 1969; Hirschi, 2004; Oetting; 1999).

Community Socialization

In modern society where alienation is more prevalent (Reckless, 1967), external social control may have less influence over controlling youth behavior due to detachments from the family (Giddens, 1991). Recommendations stemming from a government-sponsored workshop on youth exposed to violence include exploring the context in which children may be exposed to violence, including the relationship between community violence and child victimization, and other contextual factors (Analytical Sciences, 2002). Therefore, preventative measures cannot be focused solely on the family. Focusing on early risk factors alone will not suffice in altering norms that support violence. The contexts in which violence occurs need also be addressed. As shown in the present study, the victimizing effect of community-based violent socialization process may have longer-lasting effects on reactionary behaviors, including criminal behavior. The social control exerted by the community needs to have prevention efforts that focus on reducing the norms of violence, essentially delegitimizing violence-based conflict resolution. These efforts need to coincide with a staggered approach of over the life course of youth in order to reduce the possibility of on-going socialization processes that normalize violence. Such prevention measures have been hailed as a "public health imperative" (Shortt et al., 2017, p. 13).

Research has begun to show that programs emphasizing prevention tend to reduce the development of violence-based behaviors (Shortt et al., 2017). One method to implement community-based socialization that moves away from violence is education. First, there is a need for quality preschool programs. The educational and social components of preschool programs have been shown to be effective in reducing youth criminal behavior later in the life course (Schweinhart, 2007). This may be the result of developing efficient communication skills and cooperative learning (Hawkins, Smith, Hill, Kosterman, Catalano, & Abbott, 2007). In every level of schooling, implementing activities to foster problem-solving skills and combating peer pressure can reduce youth criminal behavior (Hawkins, et al., 2007). Research has shown that school programs teaching youth non-violent conflict-resolution techniques have a preventative effect on later aggressive and violent behavior among youth (Aber, Brown, & Jones, 2003). Another community-based option is peer-based organizations. These organizations, either within schools or stand-alone, can be used in the re-socialization process in order to counteract the normalizing effect of violence-based experiences. Instead, peer groups can engage positive peer pressure to provide each other with new perspectives encouraging non-violent conflict resolution and promote positive skills for success.

Structural Changes

Structural changes within nations need to be considered within crime-prevention efforts. The present study argues and supports the spillover effect of normative violent standards into socialization processes. If we want less violent societies, we need to make a conscious effort to reduce the conditions within a nation that support violence. Specifically, societies need to transmit a unified message that violence is not a healthy means in which to resolve conflict. Laws that support violent conflict resolution can be altered. This includes changing specific laws, including using physical discipline on youth and capital punishment on law offenders. Such changes take little resources, including financial, to abolish. The impact rests in societal values and perspectives. When the laws of a nation recognize subtle manifestations of violence within society as normative, this normative standard also spills over into the communities and the families that reside in those communities. Until we recognize societal acceptance of violence, we cannot begin to change norms of violence.

Prevention, then, includes altering the traditional responses of justice systems. The sanctions imposed on law violators need to be reserved strictly for the "pathological" (*cf.* Durkheim, 1977 [1914]), the most serious of law offenders. This can include reducing or eliminating prison sentences. Sanctions involving incarceration are tertiary at best: members of society who are convicted of violating the law are, in essence, put into cages to "punish" their behavior. At worst, these law offenders are being housed with other law offenders, in which the mutually shared space with limited contact to others may encourage exchanges in skills for engaging in criminal behavior. In other words, the consequences for the current sanctions imposed on individuals convicted of criminal activity may facilitate learning crime. Therefore, the structure of nations needs to depart from violent methods of social control and embrace more rehabilitative efforts so that law offenders may re-enter society as productive citizens.

This leads to a third measure to combat norms of violence: change in how nations invest in their citizenry. There needs to be a shift in the expenditure of monies. Currently, the spending of monies seems to be on military/police and justice systems (Farrell & Clark, 2004). Yet efforts on the justice system are tertiary and do not genuinely engage prevention. One of the best means to effectively control crime is primary prevention. Justice systems need to shift a large portion of the monies spent on corrections and invest more in family preservation, social programs that strengthen the family systems, and specific services to help support communities. There are calls for the preventative measures previously discussed to occur at a national level (Cullen, et al., 2007; Welsh & Farrington, 2007b) rather than a variety of individual efforts across different organizations and locations to prevent youth criminal behavior.

The current research supports the need for structural standards to move away from norms of violence. This must be a collaborative effort across various systems within the nation's structure (Greeson, Soibatian, & Houston-Koinik, 2018), including the justice systems, social service agencies, and government as a whole as well as communities and families. These steps may begin to reduce youth criminal behavior. In addition, these alterations may create a new socialization process, one of which begins a process of eradicating violence-based methods of social control.

Limitations

There are several limitations within the present study worth discussing. Studies of crime tend to be more retrospective than prospective. Respondents are asked to look back at some specific period of time to report about their prior criminal behaviors (Jolliffe et al., 2003). Retrospective studies pose challenges when attempting to measure details of criminal behavior, including frequency of minor crimes (Kazemian & Farrington, 2005) such as property crime. Memory recall of the exact frequency of criminal behavior may be inaccurate (Singleton & Straits, 1988). However, the IDVS did not use the frequency of criminal behavior as a measure. Rather, criminal behavior was measured through Likert-style response scales that capture the degree to which each respondent agreed that they had engaged in criminal behavior, including property crimes. Capturing the number of times a particular crime is committed retrospectively may be inaccurate (Maxfield & Babbie, 2010). The criminal behavior measure within the IDVS provides an estimate of the degree to which youth engaged in criminal behavior, not frequency in which criminal behavior occurred. However, it is not known how much crime each youth engaged in, and by extension the frequency of aggregate criminal behavior in each nation.

Despite the general limitation of using retrospective studies, research on violence has shown that respondents overall tend to answer accurately in retrospect (e.g., see Brewin, Andrews, & Gotlib, 1993; Kazemian & Farrington, 2005). Therefore, measures related to violence, such as violent socialization processes, should not pose as much difficulty with memory bias as measures of criminal behavior. Regardless, violent socialization processes were also measured through Likert-style response scales that capture the degree to which each respondent agreed that they had experienced violent familial socialization processes. This measure also provides an estimate rather than providing a concrete number representing the frequency in which youth had criminal behavior.

Violent socialization processes may be an imperfect measure, not being a fully representative aggregate measure of the nations in this present study. As an exploratory study, this proxy measure offers a preliminary operationalization of violent socialization in the aggregate for international research to better understand effective and ineffective methods of control over youth behavior across different nations. More research is needed to support the contention that group-level processes spill over into and influence individual-level processes. Such research would need to be conducted in a manner that does not produce ecological fallacy.

The use of a convenience sample to measure the concept of violence socialization may not be invalid. Instead, the present study indicates the possibility of construct validity by comparing these laws and the violent crime rate to violent socialization. Given that there appears to be a general lack of national-level measures on violence in other domains, including national-level attitudes, values, and behaviors, these are still proxy measures. But, these are the only national-level measures of violence consistent across the nations that are currently available.

Using samples of college students can be a limitation for criminological research. College students could possibly be part of a privileged sector of society (Cabrera & La Nasa, 2001; Kao & Tienda, 1998), particularly those youth who attend private post-secondary institutions. Additional research is recommended, with representative samples within different nations, in order to generalize results at the national level. However, criminal behavior is not exclusive to one segment of the population (Schmalleger & Bartollas, 2008). Using college students to examine criminal behavior can be important in criminological research moving forward, particularly when to create international datasets.

Researchers may have limited resources, and ability, to access the general populations of nations as a whole. The present study offers additional data for research on youth criminal behavior transnationally and provides a beginning point toward understanding the degree to which violent socialization processes may serve as control over youth criminal behavior.

Statistical conclusion validity may pose an issue for some of the findings in the present study. There are small samples of college students within some of the nations (e.g., there are only 99 cases in Iran). While the IDVS may be unique, in that there are not many studies that have such an extensive international sample, more respondents may be needed from many of the IDVS nations in order to reliably detect differences in the effects of violent familial socialization processes on individual self-reported criminal behavior (i.e., OLS regression by nation).

And finally, the present study does not account for parental reactions to youth behavior. Youth behavior can contribute to the use of socialization processes (Nurco & Lerner, 1999), and the characteristics of youth may influence the degree to which attachments form within the family (Oetting, 1999). The present study does not examine the effects of youth behavior on parental behavior. This information was not available within the IDVS dataset. Regardless, control theories do not consider the bi-directionality of parent-child relationships within the context of child development. Future research on familial socialization processes may need to consider this argument, and specifically test for the possibility of reciprocal relationships between parental behavior and youth behavior.

Although these limitations exist within the present study, this exploratory study offers an initial reference point for comparative research across different nations. While the present study cannot fully explain why children may be exposed to violence, the data presents research on methods of control that may be ineffective for preventing youth criminal behavior. At the same time, the study initiates a discussion of norms occurring within a context specific to nations. National-level norms of violence may mutually influence other domains within the nation, and these norms become the circumstance of life for youth living in that nation. Future studies should extend the findings of the present study by examining different indicators of norms within a nation that might be associated with violence, such as the presence of military/police within a nation and the current state of war/rebellion, the responses of the military/police toward perceived violence, the effects of the mass media and pop culture toward violence, and variation in criminal sanctions beyond the use of the death penalty/other methods of social control.

Final Thoughts

Social control theories seem to take the position that effective socialization is a determinate factor in preventing criminal behavior. Because many social control theorists (e.g., Gottfredson & Hirschi, 1990; Hirschi, 1969, 2004; Reckless, 1967) argue that effective familial socialization processes occur before pre-adolescence (about the age of 10–12 years), prevention of criminal behavior should begin during the early stages of childhood. As such, justice systems are ineffective in preventing youth criminal behavior because many criminal sanctions are aimed toward older youth (e.g., age 15 years or older). The results of this study support this premise: punishment through the justice systems would not effectively control all criminal behavior among youth because much family socialization occurs before youth are aware of social sanctions and legal punishments that serve to deter youth criminal behavior. And official responses to criminal behavior tend to be reactive and punitive toward individual youth, rather than focusing on the core of the problem and offering solutions (Bullock, 2011). These official responses are not generally aimed at supporting or strengthening families.

The results of the present study indicate the importance of strengthening the family in order to prevent criminal behavior. For example, it is the strength of attachments within the family which determines the degree to which youth are inculcated into the norms of society (Whitbeck, 1999). Youth exposed to deviant socialization processes, such as violent familial socialization processes, are more likely to act out with deviant behavior (Oetting, 1999). Social control theories view primary intervention within families as powerful crime control intervention. Research has supported a variety of programs in preventing youth criminal behavior. For example, Piquero, Jennings, and Farrington (2010) found that programs geared toward improving youth's ability to self-regulate their behavior were effective at reducing criminal behavior among these youth. And early intervention programs that have focused on parental management have demonstrated the ability to train parents in discipline techniques that effectively prevent criminal behavior (Przybylski, 2008; Welsh & Farrington, 2007a). Programs focused on helping youth become skilled in pro-social behavior can also prevent criminal behavior (Hawkins et al., 2007; Przybylski, 2008; Welsh & Farrington, 2007b), as well as therapeutic intervention programs targeting at-high-risk youth (Lipsey, 2009) that focus on strengthening social bonds (Bouman, De Ruiter, & Schene, 2010). Early intervention programs that specifically address youth behavior, with a focus on more rehabilitative approaches to the prevention of crime (Cullen, Vose, Jonson, & Unnever, 2007), could be established across different nations if these programs take into consideration the unique norms within the nation that may influence socialization processes both within individual families and at the societal level. All in all, current approaches to crime prevention need to address the *fundamental* issues influencing involvement in criminal behavior: ineffective familial socialization processes that contribute to youth engaging in criminal behavior. *Proactive* measures need to be taken to ensure families, in any nation, have the support they need to exert control over youth behavior and prevent criminal behavior.

In the presence of limited funding and resources available, prevention efforts should be concentrated at individual families rather than focus on communities contributing to violent socialization. Efforts aimed at preventing violence within individual families may not only reduce youth criminal behavior but also mutually influence violent socialization processes over time. With these changes in familial socialization processes, youth may then begin to take an alternative perspective toward violence with a particular focus on the latent subtleties of covert violence. Youth will eventually become the leaders in each nation. This next generation of citizenry may be able to make changes occurring at the national level, such as changes in laws that enable violence within social control practices. Politicians changing these laws have little cost to society, financially or in resources. These changes in the structural culture of a nation will then spill over into the social institutions of society and, hopefully, render norms of violence as deviant behaviors/conditions intolerable within societies. A future longitudinal study would be ideal for capturing such effects within any given nation.

Society needs to look at violent socialization in the same manner as child abuse and neglect. For example, physical discipline is violence—hitting another human being. Exposure to intimate partner violence is a form of family violence. Advising youth to use violence to resolve conflict is violence. The argument can be made that such advice could be a form of emotional manipulation, particularly if the child does not want to hit another human being. Repeated emotional manipulation is a form of emotional abuse (Crosson-Tower, 2008). Violence is harmful to the development of youth and holds long-term consequences into adulthood (e.g., see Byrne, & Lurigio, 2008; Cooper, Masi, & Vick, 2009; Kennedy, Edmonds, Dann, & Burnett, 2010; Mann, & Reynolds, 2006; Negriff, 2020; Petro, 2010). Societal perspectives on the position of children need to change. Current viewpoints that children are an extension of their parent/family and treated in a manner similar to being nothing more than chattel, seems a draconian viewpoint. Violent socialization needs to be taken seriously by systems of justice in the world. We need to raise children without a proliferation of violence. Otherwise, we will not prevent criminal behavior.

It can be argued that an indicator of civility in society is the treatment of children and youth. These are the most vulnerable members of society. To treat youth with violence is undervaluing the important role youth play in society. Youth will become adults and eventually the members of society in control of the norms. Until nations accept violence for what it is, actions or arrangements that result in harm (Iadicola & Shupe, 2003), norms of violence will remain the standard for social control and such methods to control youth behavior have a victimizing effect. Violence then becomes a vicious cycle if these youth, as adults, reproduce and reinforce norms of violence. This transmits a culture of support for violent social control. In order to truly begin prevention efforts, every member of a nation needs to recognize their role in and contribution to violent socialization processes.

Not everyone will agree with either the theoretical propositions presented in this book or the conceptualization of violence. Members of nations in which violence is a norm may be resistant to the ideas presented in this book. Having to admit that one is a member of a pro-violent nation may induce cognitive dissonance (*cf.* Aronson, 2012). The topics covered in this book are difficult to have conversations about, not only with the citizenry of a nation but also within ourselves. Topics of child maltreatment are sensitive information in many nations (Dr. Murray Straus, personal communication, May 1, 2009). Yet we must begin the challenging conversations in order to get to a point in society in which there is a standard for how we live.

Violence is a public health concern (Freire-Vargas, 2018; Satcher, 1995; Wen & Goodwin, 2016). There are consequences for violence experiences, including a negative impact on mental health (Ippen, Harris, Van Horn, & Lieberman, 2011; Lamers-Winkelman, Willemen, & Visser, 2012; Woodruff, & Lee, 2011) and criminal behavior (Demuth, & Brown, 2004; Kierkus, & Baer, 2002; Kierkus, Johnson, & Hewitt, 2010; Nash, Mujanovic, & Winfree, 2011; Rebellon, 2002). This negative impact includes acting out behaviors, which can lead to youth criminal behavior. Yet violence is not readily recognized by the citizenry of a nation unless the act of violence provides confirmation bias. Members of a nation need to examine their own contribution to violence within their society, and many may not want to recognize that they engage in violence in their day-to-day lives through socialization processes.

Change is possible. Nations can collectively choose to change the social conditions within the nation. Small changes within the structure of a nation, such laws, may spill over into the social institutions comprising those structures. Those institutions, such as the family, may then alter informal practices in socialization processes over time. With these changes, the path is paved to begin the eradication of norms of violence. More effective methods of socialization will be able to take root within families and the communities where these families reside. An underlying goal of this book is to open the dialogue about change in how expressions of violence are defined, by recognizing the various latent manifestations of violence within nations. By engaging in such dialogue, there may be reconsideration for the expressive behaviors that have not previously been considered violence, merely because those behaviors are considered a normal function in society, to be re-conceptualized. We must ask ourselves what type of society do we wish to reside in. What rights will we afford to all members of this society? Given the research presented in this book, the answer seems clear: the right to live without violence.

References

Abbey, A., Parkhill, M.R., BeShears, R., Clinton-Sherrod, A.M., & Zawacki, T. (2006). Cross-sectional predictors of sexual assault perpetration in a community sample of single men. *Aggressive Behavior, 32*(1), 54–67.

Aber, J.L., Brown, J.L., & Jones, S.M. (2003). Developmental trajectories Toward violence in middle childhood: Course, demographic differences, and response to school-based intervention. *Developmental Psychology, 39*(2), 324–348.

Aichhorn, A. (1963). *Wayward Youth.* New York: Viking.

Akers, R.L. (1990). Rational choice, deterrence, and social learning theory in criminology: The path not taken. *Journal of Criminal Law and Criminology, 81*(3), 653–676.

Akers, R.L. (2009). *Social Learning and Social Structure: A General Theory of Crime and Deviance.* Camden, NJ: Transaction Publishers.

Allison, P.D. (2002). *Missing Data.* Thousand Oaks, CA: Sage Publications, Inc.

Alvarez, A.C. & Bachman, R.D. (2017). *Violence: The Enduring Problem*, 3rd ed. Thousand Oaks, CA: Sage Publications, Inc.

American Psychiatric Association. (2013). *The Diagnostic and Statistical Manual Mental Disorders (DSM–5).* Arlington, VA: Author.

Analytical Sciences. (2002). *Children Exposed to Violence: Current Status, Gaps, and Research Priorities.* Workshop summary report. Washington, DC: National Institute of Child Health and Human Development.

Aronson, E. (2012). *The Social Animal*, 11th ed. New York: Worth Publishers.

Baker, J.O. (2010). The expression of low self-control as problematic drinking in adolescents: An integrated control perspective. *Journal of Criminal Justice, 38*(3), 237–244. DOI: 10.1016/j.jcrimjus.2010.02.011.

Bandura, A. (1977). *Social Learning Theory.* New York: General Learning Press.

Bao, W.N., Haas, A., & Pi, Y.J. (2007). Life strain, coping, and delinquency in the People's Republic of China - An empirical test of general strain theory from a matching perspective in social support. *International Journal of Offender Therapy and Comparative Criminology, 51*(1), 9–24. DOI: 10.1177/0306624X06294428.

Barnes, G.M., Hoffman, J.H., Welte, J.W., Farrell, M.P., & Dintcheff, B.A. (2006). Effects of parental monitoring and peer deviance on substance use and delinquency. *Journal of Marriage and the Family, 68*(4), 1084–1104. DOI: 10.1111/j.1741-3737.2006.00315.x.

Baron, L. & Straus, M.A. (1987). Four theories of rape: A macrosociological analysis. *Social Problems, 34*(5), 467–489. DOI: 10.2307/800542.

Baron, L. & Straus, M.A. (1988). Cultural and economic sources of homicide in the United States. *The Sociological Quarterly, 29*(3), 371–390. DOI: 10.1111/j.1533-8525.1988.tb01259.x.

Baron, L., Straus, M.A., & Jaffee, D. (1988). Legitimate violence, violent attitudes, and rape: A test of the cultural spillover theory. *Annals of the New York Academy of Sciences, 528*, 79–110. DOI: 10.1111/j.1749-6632.1988.tb50853.x.

Bauman, L.J. & Friedman, S.B. (1998). Corporal punishment. *Pediatric Clinics of North America, 45*(2), 403–414. DOI: 10.1016/S0031-3955(05)70015-8.

Beaver, K.M. (2011). The effects of genetics, the environment, and low self-control on perceived maternal and paternal socialization: Results from a longitudinal sample of twins. *Journal of Quantitative Criminology, 27*(1), 85–105. DOI: 10.1007/s10940-010-9100-z.

Beaver, K.M., Ferguson, C.J., & Lynn-Whaley, J. (2010). The association between parenting and levels of self-control: A genetically informative analysis. *Criminal Justice and Behavior, 37*(10), 1045–1065. DOI: 10.1177/0093854810374919.

Beaver, K.M. & Wright, J.P. (2007). A child effects explanation for the association between family risk and involvement in an antisocial lifestyle. *Journal of Adolescent Research, 22*(6), 640–664. DOI: 10.1177/0743558407306343.

Beaver, K.M., Wright, J.P., & Delisi, M. (2007). Self-control as an executive function: Reformulating Gottfredson and Hirschi's parental. Socialization thesis. *Criminal Justice and Behavior, 34*(10), 1345–1361. DOI: 10.1177/0093854807302049.

Bicchieri, C. & Chavez, A. (2010). Behaving as expected: Public information and fairness norms. *Journal of Behavioural Decision Making, 23*(2), 161–178. DOI: 10.2139/ssrn.1082264.

Bickel, R. (2007). *Multilevel Analysis for Applied Research*. New York: Guilford.

Bjarnason, T., Thorlindsson, T., Sigfusdottir, I.D., & Welch, M.R. (2005). Familial and religious influences on adolescent alcohol use: A multi-level study of students and school communities. *Social Forces, 84*(1), 375–390. DOI: 10.1353/sof.2005.0088.

Black, D. (2004). The geometry of terrorism. *Sociological Theory, 22*(1), 14–25. DOI: 10.1111/j.1467-9558.2004.00201.x.

Bohm, R.M. (2017). *DeathQuest: An Introduction to the Theory and Practice of Capital Punishment*, 5th ed. New York: Routledge.

Bouman, Y.H.A., de Ruiter, C., & Schene, A.H. (2010). Social ties and short-term self-reported delinquent behaviour of personality disordered forensic outpatients. *Legal and Criminological Psychology, 15*(2), 357–372. DOI: 10.1348/135532509X444528.

Bowlby, J. (1969). *Attachment and Loss*, vol. 1. New York: Basic Books.

Bowlby, J. (1973). *Attachment and Loss*, vol. 2. New York: Basic Books.

Boyd, R.J. & Higgins, G.E. (2006). Can parental support mediate the link between low self-control and deviance? *Criminal Justice Studies, 19*(3), 257–273. DOI: 10.1080/14786010600921654.

Brewin, C.R., Andrews, B., & Gotlib, I.H. (1993). Psychopathology and early experience: A reappraisal of retrospective reports. *Psychological Bulletin, 113*(1), 82–98.

Brezina, T. (1998). Adolescent maltreatment and delinquency: The question of intervening processes. *Journal of Research in Crime and Delinquency, 35*(1), 71–99. DOI: 10.1177/0022427898035001003.

Brofrenbrenner, U. (1986). Ecology of the family as a context for human development: Research Perspectives. *Developmental Psychology, 22*(6), 723–742. DOI: 0012-1649/86/S00.75.

Brown, S.L. & Rinelli, L.N. (2010). Family structure, family processes, and adolescent smoking and drinking. *Journal of Research on Adolescence, 20*(2), 259–273. DOI: 10.1111/j.1532-7795.2010.00636.x.

Bryk, A.S. & Raudenbush, S.W. (1992). *Hierarchical Linear Models: Application and Data Analysis Methods*. Newbury Park, CA: Sage Publications, Inc.

Bui, H.N. (2009). Parent-child conflicts, school troubles, and differences in delinquency across immigration generations. *Crime and Delinquency*, *55*(3), 412–441. DOI: 10.1177/0011128707306122.

Buker, H. (2011). Formation of self-control: Gottfredson and Hirschi's general theory of crime and beyond. *Aggression and Violent Behavior*, *16*(3), 265–276. DOI: 10.1016/j.avb.2011.03.005.

Bullock, K. (2011). Responding to anti-social behaviour: Analysis, interventions and the transfer of knowledge. *Crime Prevention and Community Safety*, *13*(1), 1–15. DOI: 10.1057/cpcs.2010.19.

Byrne, J.M. & Lurigio, A. (2008). Victimization and criminal behavior in adolescence and adulthood. *Victims and Offenders*, *3*(4), 319–330.

Cabrera, A.F. & La Nasa, S.M. (2001). On the path to college: Three critical tasks facing America's disadvantaged. *Research in Higher Education*, *42*(2), 119–150. DOI: 10.1023/A:1026520002362.

Cao, L., Lai, Y., & Huang, C. (2020). Exploring sources of public attitudes toward capital punishment in Taiwan. *Crime, Law, and Social Change*, *74*, 571–588. DOI: 10.1007/s10611-020-09913-2.

Capaldi, D.M., Chamberlain, P., & Patterson, G.R. (1997). Ineffective discipline and conduct problems in males: Association, late adolescent outcomes, and prevention. *Aggression and Violent Behavior*, *2*(4), 343–353.

Cappa, C. & Kahn, S.M. (2011). Understanding caregivers' attitudes towards physical punishment of children: Evidence from 34 low- and middle-income countries. *Child Abuse and Neglect*, *35*(12), 1009–1021. DOI: 10.1016/j.chiabu.2011.10.003.

Carmines, E.G., & Zeller, R.A. (1979). *Reliability and Validity Assessment*. Thousand Oaks, CA: Sage Publications, Inc.

Case, P.F. (2008). The relationship between race and criminal behavior: Challenging cultural explanations for a structural problem. *Critical Sociology*, *34*(2), 213–238. DOI: 10.1177/0896920507085513.

Champion, D.J., Merlo, A.V., & Benekos, P.J. (2015). *The Juvenile Justice System: Delinquency, Processing, and the Law*, 8th ed. Upper Saddle River, NJ: Prentice Hall.

Chen, Z.S., Williams, K.D., Fitness, J., & Newton, N.C. (2008). When hurt will not heal: Exploring the capacity to relive social and physical pain. *Psychological Science*, *19*(8), 789–795. DOI: 10.1111/j.1467-9280.2008.02158.x.

Church, W.T., Wharton, T., & Taylor, J.K. (2009). An examination of differential association and social control theory: Family systems and delinquency. *Youth Violence and Juvenile Justice*, 7(1), 3–15. DOI: 10.1177/1541204008324910.

Cloward, R.A. & Ohlin, L.E. ([1960]2001). *Delinquency and Opportunity: A Study of Delinquent Gangs*. Oxon, UK: Routledge.

Cohen, A.K. (1955). *Delinquent Boys: The Culture of the Gang*. Glencoe, IL. Free Press.

Cohen, A.K. & Short, J.F. (1958). Research in delinquent subcultures. *Journal of Social Issues*, *14*(3), 20–37.

Cohn, E.S. & White, S.O. (1990). *Legal Socialization: A Study of Norms and Rules*. New York: Springer.

Conejero, I., Olié, E., Calati, R., Ducasse, D., & Courtet, P. (2018). Psychological pain, depression, and suicide: Recent evidences and future directions. *Current Psychiatry Reports*, *20*(5), 33–42. DOI: 10.1007/s11920-018-0893-z.

Cooper, J.L., Masi, R., & Vick, J. (2009). Social and emotional development in early childhood: What every policymaker should know. New York: National Center for Children in Poverty. Columbia University. http://www.nccp.org/publications/pdf/text_882.pdf.

Cornell Center on the Death Penalty Worldwide. (2020). Death penalty database. https://dpw.pointjupiter.co/search.cfm.

Crosson-Tower, C. (2008). *Understanding Child Abuse and Neglect*, 7th ed. Boston, MA: Allyn and Bacon.

Crowne, D.P. & Marlowe, F. (1960). A new scale of social desirability independent of psychopathology. *Journal of Consulting Psychology, 24*, 349–354.

Crump, T.G. (2017). Is the criminal justice or criminology master's degree necessary? *ACJS Today, XLII*(5), 1–3. https://cdn.ymaws.com/acjs.site-ym.com/resource/resmgr/acjstoday/ACJS_Today_November_2017.pdf.

Cullen, F.T., Vose, B.A., Lero Jonson, C.N., & Unnever, J.D. (2007). Public Support for early intervention: Is child saving a "habit of the heart"? *Victims and Offenders, 2*(2), 109–124. DOI: 10.1080/15564880701263015.

Curran, D.J. & Renzetti, C.M. (1994). *Theories of Crime*. Needham Heights, MA: Allyn & Bacon.

Dawson, J. & Straus, M.A. (2011). Gender equality in society and male predominance in crime by university students in thirty-two national settings. *The Open Criminology Journal, 4*, 10–23.

De Li, S. (2004). The impacts of self-control and social bonds on juvenile delinquency in a national sample of midadolescents. *Deviant Behavior, 25*(4), 351–373. DOI: 10.1080/01639620490441236.

Death Penalty Information Center. (2012). Death penalty worldwide. http://www.deathpenaltyworldwide.org/index.cfm.

DeGue, S., DiLillo, D., & Scalora, M. (2010). Are all perpetrators alike? Comparing risk factors for sexual coercion and aggression. *Sexual Abuse: A Journal of Research and Treatment, 22*(4), 402–426. DOI: 10.1177/1079063210372140.

Delaney, A.X. (2015). Violent socialization and youth violence across different nations: International variations in familial and contextual factors. *Contemporary Perspectives in Family Research, 9*, 129–151.

Delaney, A.X. (forthcoming, 2021a). Intersections of childhood victimization experiences, gender, and power: The makings for sexual coercion? *International Criminal Justice Review*. DOI: 10.1177/1057567720982655.

Delaney, A.X. (forthcoming, 2021b). A transnational comparison of the victimizing effect of violent socialization on sexually coercive behaviors towards intimate partners. *International Journal of Offender Therapy and Comparative Criminology*.

Demuth, S. & Brown, S. (2004). Family structure, family processes, and adolescent delinquency: The significance of parental absence versus parental gender. *Journal of Research in Crime and Delinquency, 41*(1), 58–81. DOI: 10.1177/0022427803256236.

Dillon, F.R., Pantin, H., Robbins, M.S., & Szapocznik, J. (2008). Exploring the role of parental monitoring of peers on the relationship between family functioning and delinquency in the lives of African American and Hispanic adolescents. *Crime and Delinquency, 54*(1), 65–94. DOI: 10.1177/0011128707305744.

Douglas, E.M. & Straus, M.A. (2006). Assault and injury of dating partners by university students in 19 countries and its relation to corporal punishment experienced as a child. *European Journal of Criminology, 3*(3), 293–318. DOI: 10.1177/1477370806065584.

Dufour, S., Clément, M., Chamberland, C., & Dubeau, D. (2011). Child abuse in a disciplinary context: A typology of violent family environments. *Journal of Family Violence, 26*(8), 595–606.

Durkheim, É. (1977 (1914)) Steven Lukes editors. *Rules of Sociological Method and Selected Texts on Sociology and Its Method*. New York: The Free Press.

Edwards, J.E. (1996). A measurement of delinquency differences between a delinquent and a nondelinquent sample: What are the implications? *Adolescence, 31*(124), 973–989.

Eller, J.D. (2006). Violence and Culture: A Cross-Cultural and Interdisciplinary Approach. Belmont, CA: Wadsworth.

Ellickson, P.L. & Morton, S.C. (1999). Identifying adolescents at risk for hard drug use: Racial/ethnic variations. *Journal of Adolescent Health, 25*(6), 382–395.

Ember, C.R. & Ember, M. (1994). War. War, socialization, and interpersonal violence: A cross-cultural study. *The Journal of Conflict Resolution, 38*(4), 620–646. DOI: 10.2307/174332.

Erikson, E.H. (1950). *Childhood and Society*. New York: Norton.

Eriksson, M. (2010). Children who "witness" violence as crime victims and changing family law in Sweden. *Journal of Child Custody, 17*(2), 93–116. DOI: 10.1080/15379418.2010.508258.

Farrell, G. & Clark, K. (2004). What does the world spend on criminal justice? *The European* Institute for Crime Prevention and Control. https://www.heuni.fi/material/attachments/heuni/papers/6KtlkZMtL/HEUNI_papers_20.pdf.

Farrington, D.P. (2003). Developmental and life-course criminology: Key theoretical and empirical issues-the 2002 Sutherland award address. *Criminology, 41*(2), 221–225. DOI: 10.1111/j.1745-9125.2003.tb00987.x.

Feder, J., Levant, R.F., & Dean, J. (2010). Boys and violence: A gender-informed analysis. *Psychology of Violence, 1*(S), 3–12.

Feld, S.L. & Straus, M.A. (1989). Escalation and desistance of wife assault in marriage. *Criminology, 27*(1), 141–162. DOI: 10.1111/j.1745-9125.1989.tb00866.x.

Felitti, V.J., Anda, R.F., Nordenberg, D., Williamson, D.F., Spitz, A.M., Edwards, V., Koss, M.P., & Marks, J.S. (1998). Relationship of childhood abuse and household dysfunction to many of the leading causes of death in adults. The Adverse Childhood Experiences (ACE) Study. *American Journal of Preventive Medicine, 14*(4), 245–258.

Fine, A., Mahler, A., Stein, L., Frick, P.J., & Cauffman, E. (2017). Individual in context: The role of impulse control on the association between the home, school, and neighborhood developmental contexts and adolescent delinquency. *Journal of Youth and Adolescence, 46*(7), 1488–1502. DOI: 10.1007/s10964-016-0565-4.

Finkelhor, D. & Wells, M. (2003). Improving data systems about juvenile victimization in the United States. *Child Abuse and Neglect, 27*(1), 77–102. DOI: 10.1016/s0145-2134(02)00508-2.

Fischer, C. (1995). The subcultural theory of urbanism: A twentieth year assessment. *American Journal of Sociology, 101*(3), 543–577.

Fonagy, P., Target, M., Steele, M., Steele, H., Leigh, T., Levinson, A., & Kennedy, R. (1997). Morality, disruptive behavior, borderline personality disorder, crime, and their relationships to security of attachment. In: L. Atkinson & K.J. Zucker (Eds.), *Attachment and Psychopathology* (pp. 223–274). New York: The Guiliford Press.

Forbes, G.B. & Adams-Curtis, L.E. (2001). Experiences with sexual coercion in college males and females: Role of family conflict, sexist attitudes, acceptance of rape myths, self-esteem, and the big-five personality factors. *Journal of Interpersonal Violence, 16*(9), 865–889. DOI: 10.1177/088626001016009002.

Forjuoh, S.N. & Zwi, A.B. (1998). Violence among children and adolescents: International perspectives. *Pediatric Clinics of North America, 45*, 2–426.

Fowler, F.J. (2009). *Survey Research Methods*, 4th ed. Thousand Oaks, CA: Sage Publications, Inc.

Freire-Vargas, L. (2018). Violence as a public health crisis. *AMA Journal of Ethics, 20*(1), 25–28. DOI: 10.1001/journalofethics.2018.20.1.fred1-1801.

Furstenberg, F.F. (1993). How families manage risk and opportunity in dangerous neighborhoods. In: W.J. Wilson (Ed.), *Sociology and the Public Agenda* (pp. 231–258). Newbury Park, CA: Sage Publications, Inc.

Gabarino, J. (1997). Educating children in a socially toxic environment. *Educational Leadership, 54*, 12–16.

Gagné, M.-H., Tourigny, M., Joly, J., & Pouliot-Lapointe, J. (2007). Predictors of adult attitudes toward corporal punishment of children. *Journal of Interpersonal Violence, 22*(10), 1285–1304. DOI: 10.1177/0886260507304550.

Gàmez-Guadix, M., Straus, M.A., & Hershberger, S. (2011). Childhood and adolescent victimization and perpetration of sexual coercion by male and female university students. *Deviant Behavior, 32*(8), 712–742. DOI: 10.1.1.194.2065.

Gartner, R. (1993). Methodological issues in cross-cultural large-survey research on violence. *Violence and Victims, 8*(3), 199–213.

Gershoff, E.T. (2008). Report on physical punishment in the United States: What research tells us about its effects on children. Columbus, OH: Center for Effective Discipline. www.phoenixchildrens.com/ pdfs/principles_and_practices-of_effective_discipline.pdf.

Gershoff, E.T. & Bitensky, S.H. (2007). The case against corporal punishment of children: Converging evidence from social science research and international human rights law and implications for US public policy. *Psychology, Public Policy and Law, 13*(4), 231–272. DOI: 10.1037/1076-8971.13.4.231.

Gibbs, J.J., Giever, D., & Martin, J.S. (1998). Parental management and self-control: An empirical test of Gottfredson and Hirschi's general theory. *Journal of Research in Crime and Delinquency, 35*(1), 40–70.

Gibson, C.L., Morris, S.Z., & Beaver, K.M. (2009). Secondary exposure to violence during childhood and adolescence: Does neighborhood context matter? *Justice Quarterly, 26*(1), 30–57. DOI: 10.1080/07418820802119968.

Giddens, A. (1991). *Modernity and Self-Identity: Self and Society in the Late Modern Age*. Stanford, CA: Stanford University Press.

Global Initiative to End All Corporal Punishment of Children (2012). *Legality of Corporal Punishment Worldwide*. http://www.endcorporalpunishment.org/pages/frame.html.

Goddard, H.W., Goff, B.G., Melancon, M.V., & Huebner, A.J. (2000). Profiles of delinquency: A comparison of delinquent behavioral groups. *Journal of Social Behavior and Personality, 15*, 19–50.

Goetting, A. (1994). The parenting–crime connection. *Journal of Primary Prevention, 14*(3), 169–186.

Goffman, E. (1959). *The Presentation of Self in Everyday Life*. New York: Anchor Books.

Goldstein, H. (1988). *Multilevel Statistical Models*. New York: John Wiley.

Gorman-Smith, D. & Tolan, P.H. (1998). The role of exposure to community violence and developmental problems among inner-city youth. *Development and Psychology, 74*, 101–116.

Gottfredson, M.R. (2005). The empirical status of control theory in criminology. In: F.T. Cullen, J.P. Wright, & K.R. Blevins (Eds.), *Taking Stock: The Status of Criminological Theory* (pp. 77–100). New Brunswick, NJ: Transaction.

Gottfredson, M.R. & Hirschi, T. (1990). *A General Theory of Crime*. Stanford, CA: Stanford University Press.

Grasmick, H.G., Tittle, C.R., Bursik, R.J., & Arneklev, B.J. (1993). Testing the core empirical implications of Gottfredson and Hirschi's general theory of crime. *Journal of Research in Crime and Delinquency*, *30*(1), 5–29.

Greenfield, P.M., Flores, A., Davis, H., & Salimkhan, G. (2008). What happens when parents and nannies come from different cultures? Comparing the caregiving belief systems of nannies and their employers. *Journal of Applied Developmental Psychology*, *29*(4), 326–336. DOI: 10.1016/j.appdev.2008.04.002.

Greeson, M.R., Soibatian, C., & Houston-Koinik, J.D. (2018). The influence of community sociocultural context on creating an effective, coordinated response to sexual assault. *Psychology of Women Quarterly*, *42*(4), 445–460.

Greven, P.J. (1992). *Spare the Child*. New York: Random House, Inc.

Grimes, D.A. & Schulz, K.F. (2005). Compared to what? Finding controls for case-control studies. *The Lancet*, *365*(9468), 1429–1433.

Gumbrecht, J. (2011, November 9). In Sweden, a generation of kids who've never been spanked. *CNN*. http://articles.cnn.com/2011-11-09/world/world_sweden-punishment-ban_1_corporal-punishment-elizabeth-gershoff-parents?_s=PM:WORLD.

Hagan, J. & McCarthy, B. (1997). Anomie, social capital, and street criminology. In: N. Passas & R. Agnew (Eds.), *The Future of Anomie Theory* (pp. 124–141). Boston, MA: Northeastern University Press.

Hamby, S., Finkelhor, D., Turner, H., & Ormrod, R. (2011). *Children's Exposure to Intimate Partner Violence and Other Family Violence*. (OJJDP Publication No. 232272). Washington, DC: U.S. Government Printing Office. http://www.ncbi.nlm.nih.gov/pubmed/232272.

Hamilton, L.C. (1992). *Regression with Graphics*. Pacific Grove, CA: Brooks/Cole.

Hamilton, L.C. (2013). *Statistics with Stata*: Version 12, 8th ed. College Station, TX: StataCorp LP.

Hawkins, J.D., Smith, B.H., Hill, K.G., Kosterman, R., Catalano, R.F., & Abbott, R.D. (2007). Promoting social development and preventing health and behavior problems during the elementary grades: Results from the Seattle Social Development Project. *Victims and Offenders*, *2*(2), 161–181.

Hayes, A.F. (2006). A primer on multilevel modeling. *Human Communication Research*, *32*(4), 385–410. DOI: 10.1111/j.1468-2958.2006.00281.x.

Hayhurst, L.M., Sundstrom, L.M., & Emma Arksey, E. (2018). Navigating norms: Charting gender-based violence prevention and sexual health rights through global-local sport for development and peace relations in Nicaragua. *Sociology of Sport Journal*, *35*(3), 277–288. DOI: 10.1123/ssj.2017-0065.

Heath, L., Kruttsschnitt, C., & Ward, D. (1986). Television and violent criminal behavior: Beyond the Bobo doll. *Victims and Violence*, *1*(3), 177–190.

Herrenkohl, R.C., Herrenkohl, E.C., Egolf, B.P., & Wu, P. (1991). The developmental consequences of child abuse: The Lehigh longitudinal study. In: R.H.J. Starr & D.A. Wolfe (Eds.), *The Effects of Child Abuse and Neglect: Issues and Research* (pp. 57–81). New York: Guilford.

Herrenkohl, T.I., Huang, B., Tajima, E.A., & Whitney, S.D. (2003). Examining the link between child abuse and youth violence: An analysis of mediating mechanisms. *Journal of Interpersonal Violence, 18*(10), 1189–1208. DOI: 10.1177/0886260503255558.

Heywood, C. (2010). *A History of Childhood*. Malden, MA: Polity Press.

Hirschi, T. (1969). *The Causes of Delinquency*. New York: Oxford Press.

Hirschi, T. (2004). Self-control and crime. In: R.F. Baumeister & K.D. Vohs (Eds.), *Handbook of Self-Regulation: Research, Theory, and Applications* (pp. 537–552). New York: Guilford Publications.

Hurrelman, K. (1990). Parents, peers, teachers, and other significant partners in adolescence. *International Journal of Adolescence and Youth, 2*(3), 211–236.

Iadicola, P. (2012). Violence: Definitions, spheres, and principles. In: D.W. Harper, L. Voigt, & W.E. Thornton (Eds.), Violence: Do *We* Know *It When We* See *It*? (pp. 7–26). Durham, NC: Carolina Academic Press.

International Social Survey Programme. (2019, June). *ISSP 2012 - "Family and Changing Gender Roles IV" - ZA No. 5900*. Gesis: Leibniz Institute for Social Sciences. https://www.gesis.org/en/issp/modules/issp-modules-by-topic/family-and-changing-gender-roles/2012

Ippen, C.G., Harris, W.W., Van Horn, P., & Lieberman, A.F. (2011). Traumatic and stressful events in early childhood: Can treatment help those at highest risk? *Child Abuse and Neglect, 35*(7), 504–513.

Jackson, S., Thompson, R.A., Christiansen, E.H., Colman, R.A., Wyatt, J., Buckendahl, C.W., Wilcox, B.L., & Peterson, R.L. (1999). Predicting abuse-prone parental attitudes and discipline practices in a nationally representative sample. *Child Abuse and Neglect, 23*(1), 15–29.

Janson, S., Långberg, B., & Svensson, B. (2011). Sweden: A 30-year ban on physical punishment of children. In: J.E. Durrant & A.B. Smith (Eds.), *Global Pathways to Abolishing Physical Punishment: Realizing Children's Rights* (pp. 241–255). New York: Routledge.

Jensen, G.F. (1973). Inner containment and delinquency. *The Journal of Criminal Law and Criminology, 64*(4), 464–470.

Johnson, E.H., & Barak-Glantz, I.L. (1983). Introduction. In E.H. Johnson and I.L. Barak-Glantz (Eds.), *Comparative Criminology* (pp. 1–18). Thousand Oaks, CA: Sage Publications, Inc.

Johnson, V. & Pandina, R.J. (1991). Effects of the family environment on adolescent substance use, delinquency, and coping styles. *American Journal on Alcohol Abuse, 17*(1), 71–88.

Johnson, W.L., Giordano, P.C., Manning, W.D., & Longmore, M.A. (2011). Parent–child relations and offending during young adulthood. *Journal of Youth and Adolescence, 40*(7), 786–799. DOI: 10.1007/s10964-010-9591-9.

Jolliffe, D., Farrington, D.P., Hawkins, J.D., Catalano, R.F., Hill, K.G., & Kosterman, R. (2003). Predictive, concurrent, prospective and retrospective validity of self-reported delinquency. *Criminal Behavior and Mental Health, 13*(3), 179–197. DOI: 10.1002/cbm.541.

Jones, K. & Subramanian, V.S. (2019). *Developing Multilevel Models for Analysing Contextuality, Heterogeneity and Change Using MLwiN 3*, Vol. 1. Bristol, UK: Centre for Multilevel Modelling.

Jung, H., Herrenkohl, T.I., Lee, J.O., Hemphill, S.A., Heerde, J.A., & Skinner, M.L. (2017). Gendered pathways from child abuse to adult crime through internalizing and externalizing behaviors in childhood and adolescence. *Journal of Interpersonal Violence, 32*(18), 2724–2750. DOI: 10.1177/0886260515596146.

Kahn, A. & Paluzzi, P. (2006). Boys will be boys: Understanding the impact of child maltreatment and family violence on the sexual, reproductive, and parenting behaviors of young men. Healthy Teen Network. https://www.healthyteennetwork.org/wp-content/uploads/2014/10/BoysWillBeBoys.pdf.

Kain, G.F. & Recinella, D. (2017). Retribution and capital punishment: *"It's in the Bible, isn't it?"* In Robert M. Bohm & Gavin Lee (Eds.), *Routledge Handbook on Capital Punishment.* New York: Routledge. DOI: 10.4324/9781315624723-9.

Kao, G. & Tienda, M. (1998). Educational aspirations of minority youth. *American Journal of Education, 106*(3), 349–384.

Kasarda, J.D. & Janowitz, M. (1974). Community attachment in mass society. *American Sociological Review, 39*(3), 328–339.

Kazemian, L. & Farrington, D.P. (2005). Comparing the validity of prospective, retrospective, and official onset for different offending categories. *Journal of Quantitative Criminology, 21*(2), 127–147. DOI: 10.1007/s10940-005-2489-0.

Keller, H., Otto, H., Lamm, B., Yovsi, R.D., & Kartner, J. (2008). The timing of verbal/vocal communications between mothers and their infants: A longitudinal cross-cultural comparison. *Infant Behavior and Development, 31*(2), 217–226. DOI: 10.1016/j.infbeh.2007.10.001.

Kelley, J. & De Graaf, N.D. (1997). National context, parental socialization, and religious belief: Results from 15 nations. *American Sociological Review, 62*(4), 639–659. DOI: 10.2307/2657431.

Kendall, D. (2010). *Sociology in Our Times: Essentials*, 7th ed. Belmont, CA: Wadsworth Cengage Learning.

Kennedy, T.D., Edmonds, W.A., Dann, K.T., & Burnett, K.F. (2010). The clinical and adaptive features of young offenders with histories of child-parent violence. *Journal of Family Violence, 25*(5), 509–520.

Kerig, P.K. (2019). Linking childhood trauma exposure to adolescent justice involvement: The concept of posttraumatic risk-seeking. *Clinical Psychology: Science and Practice, 26*(3), e12280. DOI: 10.1111/cpsp.12280.

Kierkus, C.A. & Baer, D. (2002). A social control explanation of the relationship between family structure and delinquent behaviour. *Canadian Journal of Criminology, 44*, 425–458.

Kierkus, C.A., Johnson, B.R., & Hewitt, J.D. (2010). Cohabiting, family and community stressors, selection, and juvenile delinquency. *Criminal Justice Review, 35*(4), 393–411. DOI: 10.1177/0734016810379338.

Knowles, C. (1996). *Family Boundaries: The Invention of Normality and Dangerousness.* Orchard Park, NY: Broadview Press.

Kobayashi, E., Vazsonyi, A.T., Chen, P., & Sharp, S.F. (2010). Dimensionality and generalizability in Japan and the United States: A culturally nuanced test of Gottfredson and Hirschi's general theory. *International Criminal Justice Review, 20*, 112–131. DOI: 10.1177/1057567710368362.

LaFree, G. (2005). Evidence for elite convergence in cross-national homicide victimization trends, 1956 to 2000. *The Sociological Quarterly, 46*(1), 191–211. DOI: 10.1111/j.1533-8525.2005.00009.x.

Lamers-Winkelman, F., Willemen, A.M., & Visser, M. (2012). Adverse childhood experiences of referred children exposed to intimate partner violence: Consequences for their wellbeing. *Child Abuse and Neglect, 36*(2), 166–179.

Lansford, J.E., Chang, L., Dodge, K.A., Malone, P.S., Oburu, P., Palmérus, K., Quinn, N., Pastorelli, C., Bombi, A.S., Zelli, A., Tapanya, S., Chaudhary, N., Deater-Deckard,

K., Manke, B., & Quinn, N. (2005). Physical discipline and children's adjustment: Cultural normativeness as a moderator. *Child Development, 76*(6), 1234–1246. DOI: 10.1111/j.1467-8624.2005.00847.x.

Lansford, J.E. & Dodge, K.A. (2008). Cultural norms for adult corporal punishment of children and societal rates of endorsement and use of violence. *Parenting: Science and Practice, 8*(3), 257–270. DOI: 10.1080/15295190802204843.

Lareau, A. (2002). Invisible inequality: Social class and childrearing in black families and white families. *American Sociological Review, 67*(5), 747–776.

Lareau, A. (2003). *Unequal Childhoods: Class, Race and Family Life.* Berkeley, CA: University of California Press.

Laub, J.H. & Sampson, R.J. (2003). *Shared Beginnings, Divergent Lives: Delinquent Boys to Age 70.* Cambridge, MA: Harvard University Press.

Lee, M.R. & Ousey, G.O. (2012). Southern violence: A contemporary overview. In: D.W. Harper, W.E. Thornton, & L. Voigt (Eds.), *Violence: Do We Know It When We See It? A reader* (pp. 115–128). Durham, NC: Carolina Academic Press.

Lee, R.M. (1993). *Doing Research on Sensitive Topics.* Thousand Oaks, CA: Sage Publications, Inc.

Lee, Y. & Kim, S. (2011). Childhood maltreatment in South Korea: Retrospective study. *Child Abuse and Neglect, 35*(12), 1037–1044. DOI: 10.1016/j.chiabu.2011.09.005.

Levinson, D. (1989). *Family Violence in Cross-Cultural Perspective.* Newbury Park, CA: Sage Publications, Inc.

Lipsey, M.W. (1990). *Design Sensitivity: Statistical Power for Experimental Research.* Thousand Oaks, CA: Sage Publications, Inc..

Lipsey, M.W. (2009). The primary factors that characterize effective interventions with juvenile offenders: A meta-analytic overview. *Victims and Offenders, 2*(2), 124–147. DOI: 10.1080/15564880802612573.

Lipsey, M.W. & Derzon, J.H. (1998). Predictors of violent or serious delinquency in adolescence and early adulthood: A synthesis of longitudinal research. In: R. Loeber & D.P. Farrington (Eds.), *Serious & Violent Juvenile Offenders: Risk Factors and Successful Interventions* (pp. 86–105). Thousand Oaks, CA: Sage Publications, Inc.

Loeber, R. & Dishion, T. (1983). Early predictors of male delinquency: A review. *Psychological Bulletin, 94*(1), 68–99.

Loeber, R. & Stouthamer-Loeber, M. (1986). Family factors as correlates and predictors of juvenile conduct problems and delinquency. In: M. Tonry & N. Morris (Eds.), *Crime and Justice: A Review of Research* (pp. 29–149). Chicago, IL: University of Chicago Press.

Luke, D.A. (2004). *Multilevel Modeling.* Thousand Oaks, CA: Sage Publications, Inc.

Luthar, S.S. & Goldstein, A.S. (2008). Substance use and related behaviors among suburban late adolescents: The importance of perceived parent containment. *Development and Psychopathology, 20*(2), 591–614. DOI: 10.1017/S0954579408000291.

Lyndon, A.E., White, J.W., & Kadlec, K.M. (2007). Manipulation and force as sexual coercion tactics: Conceptual and empirical differences. *Aggressive Behavior, 33*(4), 291–303. DOI: 10.1002/ab.20200.

Lysova, A. & Straus, M.A. (2019). Intimate partner violence: A multinational test of cultural spillover theory. *Journal of Interpersonal Violence, 0*(00), 1-29. DOI: 10.1177/0886260519839421.

Mackie, G. & LeJeune, J. (2009). Social dynamics of abandonment of harmful practices: A new look at the theory. Innocenti Working Paper 2009-06: Florence, Italy. http://www

.polisci.ucsd.edu/~gmackie/documents/UNICEF.pdf. UNICEF Innocenti Research Centre.

Mann, E.A. & Reynolds, A.J. (2006). Early intervention and juvenile delinquency prevention: Evidence from the Chicago longitudinal study. *Social Work Research, 30*(3), 153–167.

Margolin, G. & Gordis, E.B. (2000). The effect of family and community violence on children. *Annual Review of Psychology, 51*, 445–479. DOI: 10.1146/annurev.psych.51.1.445.

Matherne, M.M. & Thomas, A. (2001). Family environment as a predictor of adolescent delinquency. *Adolescence, 36*(144), 655–664.

Matsueda, R. (2013). The macro – Micro problem in criminology revisited. *The Criminologist, 38*(1), 1–7. https://www.asc41.com/Criminologist/leadArticleIndex.html.

Mattingly, M.J. & Straus, M.A. (2008). Violence socialization and approval of violence: A world perspective on gender differences and American violence. Paper presented at the American Society of Criminology. St. Louis, MO. https://cola.unh.edu/family-research-laboratory.

Maxfield, M.G. & Babbie, E. (2010). *Research Methods for Criminal Justice and Criminology*. Belmont, CA: Thomson Wadworth.

Mazerolle, l., Wickes, R., & McBroom, J. (2010). Community variations in violence: The role of social ties and collective efficacy in comparative context. *Journal of Research in Crime and Delinquency, 20*(1), 3–30. DOI: 10.1177/0022427809348898.

Mead, G.H. (1934). *Mind, Self, and Society*. Chicago, IL: University of Chicago Press.

Merriam-Webster. (2020, January 8). Force. *Merriam-Webster Dictionary*. https://www.merriam-webster.com/dictionary/force.

Messner, S.F. & Rosenfeld, R. (2008). Institutional anomie theory. In: Francis T. Cullen, John Wright, & Kristie Blevins (Eds.), *Taking Stock: The Status of Criminological Theory* (pp. 127–148). New York: Routledge. DOI: 10.4324/9781315130620.

Mfonobong, D.U., Bassey, S.A., & Okpe, T.A. (2019). Kantian and utilitarian ethics on capital punishment. *Budapest International Research and Critics Institute-Journal, 2*(2), 28–35.

Midlarsky, E., Bryan, J.H., & Brickman, P. (1973). Aversive approval: Interactive effects of modeling and reinforcement on altruistic behavior. *Child Development, 44*(2), 321–328.

Miller, W.B. (1998). Lower class culture as a generating milieu of gang delinquency. In: F.P. Williams & M.D. McShane (Eds.), *Criminology Theory: Selected Classic Readings*, 2nd ed. (pp. 163–179). Cincinnati, OH: Anderson.

Miller-Perrin, C.L. & Perrin, R.D. (1999). *Child Maltreatment: An Introduction*. Thousand Oaks, CA: Sage Publications, Inc.

Milletich, R.J., Kelley, M.L., Doane, A.N., & Pearson, M.R. (2010). Exposure to interparental violence and childhood physical and emotional abuse as related to physical aggression in undergraduate dating relationships. *Journal of Family Violence, 25*(7), 627–637.

Moffatt, M. (1991). College life: Undergraduate culture and higher education. *The Journal of Higher Education, 61*, 44–61.

Montague, A. (1978). *Learning Non-Aggression: The Experience of Non-Literate Societies*. New York: Oxford University Press.

Morrall, P. (2006). Murder and society: Why commit murder? *Criminal Justice Matters, 66*(1), 36–37. https://www.crimeandjustice.org.uk/publications/cjm/article/murder-and-society-why-commit-murder.

Morris, R.G., Gerber, J., & Menard, S. (2011). Social bonds, self-control, and adult criminality: A Nationally representative assessment of Hirschi's revised self-control theory. *Criminal Justice and Behavior, 38*(6), 584–599. DOI: 10.1177/0093854811402453.

Morrongiello, B.A., Corbett, M., & Bellissimo, A. (2008). "Do as I say, not as I do": Family influences on children's safety and risk behaviors. *Health Psychology, 27*(4), 498–503.

Nash, J.K., Mujanovic, E., & Winfree, L.T. (2011). Protective effects of parental monitoring on offending in victimized youth in Bosnia and Herzegovina. *Child and Youth Services, 32*(3), 224–242.

Negriff, S. (2020). ACEs are not equal: Examining the relative impact of household dysfunction versus childhood maltreatment on mental health in adolescence. *Social Science and Medicine, 245*(112696), 1–8. DOI: 10.1016/j.socscimed.2019.112696.

Nesse, R.M. & Schulkin, J. (2019). An evolutionary medicine perspective on pain and its disorders. *Philosophical Transactions of the Royal Society Series B, 374*(1785). DOI: 10.1098/rstb.2019.0288.

Nurco, D.N., Lerner, M. (1999). A complementary perspective to primary socialization theory. *Substance Use and Misuse, 34*(7), 993–1003. DOI: 10.3109/10826089909039391.

Nye, F.I. & Weeks, H.A. (1956). The rejected parent and delinquency. *Marriage and Family Living, 18*(4), 291–300.

Oetting, E.R. (1999). Primary socialization theory: Developmental stages, spirituality, government institutions, sensation seeking, and theoretical implications. *Substance Use and Misuse, 34*(7), 947–982. DOI: 10.3109/10826089909039389.

Oetting, E.R. & Donnermeyer, J.F. (2009). Primary socialization theory: The etiology of drug use and deviance. I. *Substance Use and Misuse, 33*(4), 995–1026. DOI: 10.3109/10826089809056252.

https://www.ohchr.org/EN/HRBodies/CRC/Study/Pages/StudyViolenceChildren.aspx.

Ohene, S.A., Ireland, M., McNeely, C., & Borowsky, I.W. (2006). Parental expectations, physical punishment, and violence among adolescents who score positive on a psychosocial screening test in primary care. *Pediatrics, 117*(2), 441–447. DOI: 10.1542/peds.2005-0421.

Ojo, O.O., Akintomide, A.G., & Omoyemiju, M.A. (2011). Parental perception and attitude to children's violent acts in Ife central local government area secondary schools. *Edo Journal of Counselling, 4*(1&2), 103–115.

O'Keefe, D.J. (2007). Potential conflicts between normatively-responsible advocacy and successful social influence: Evidence from persuasion effects research. *Argumentation, 21*(2), 151–163. DOI: 10.1007/s10503-007-9046-y.

Olds, D.L. (2007). Preventing crime with prenatal and infancy support of parents: The Nurse-Family Partnership. *Victims and Offenders, 2*(2), 205–225.

Ormrod, J.E. (1999). *Human Learning*, 3rd ed. Sydney, NSW: Merrill, Prentice Hall Australia Pty Ltd.

Ousey, G.C. & Lee, M.R. (2010). The southern culture of violence and homicide type differentiation: An analysis across cities and time points. *Homicide Studies, 14*(3), 268–295.

Palmeri Sams, D. & Turcotte, S.D. (2004). Empathy, exposure to community violence, and use of violence among urban, at-risk adolescents. *Child and Youth Care Forum, 33*(1), 33–50. DOI: 10.1023/B:CCAR.0000013756.88343.5f.

Parker, J.S. & Benson, M.J. (2004). Parent-adolescent relations and adolescent functioning: Self-esteem, substance abuse, and delinquency. *Adolescence, 39*(155), 519–530.

Paternoster, R. & Pogarsky, G. (2009). Rational choice, agency, and thoughtfully reflective decision making: The short and long-term consequences of making good choices. *Journal of Quantitative Criminology*, *25*(2), 103–127.

Payne, B.K. & Chappell, A. (2009). Using student samples in criminological research. *Journal of Criminal Justice Education*, *19*(2), 175–192. DOI: 10.1080/10511250802137226.

Payne, B.K., Higgins, G.E., & Blackwell, B. (2010). Exploring the link between self-control and partner violence: Bad parenting or general criminals. *Journal of Criminal Justice*, *38*(5), 1015–1021. DOI: 10.1016/j.jcrimjus.2010.07.003.

Petersen, A.C., Joseph, J., & Feit, M. (Eds.). (2014). *New Directions in Child Abuse and Neglect Research*. Washington, DC: National Academies Press.

Petro, J. (2010). Increasing collaboration and coordination of the child welfare and juvenile justice systems to better serve dual jurisdiction youth: A literature review. Washington, DC: Welfare League of America. http://www.cwla.org/programs/juvenilejustice/jjlit review.pdf.

Pinheiro, P.S. (2006). Rights of the child: Report of the independent expert for the United Nations study on violence against children. New York: United Nations. http://www .unicef.org/violencestudy/reports/SG_violencestudy_en.pdf.

Piquero, A.R. & Bouffard, J.A. (2007). Something old, something new: A preliminary investigation of Hirschi's redefined self-control. *Justice Quarterly*, *24*(1), 1–27. DOI: 10.1080/07418820701200935.

Piquero, A.R., Jennings, W.G., & Farrington, D.P. (2010). On the malleability of self-control: Theoretical and policy implications regarding a general theory of crime. *Justice Quarterly*, *27*(6), 803–834. DOI: 10.1080/07418820903379628.

Pittman, L.D. & Chase-Lansdale, P.L. (2001). African American adolescent girls in impoverished communities: Parenting style and adolescent outcomes. *Journal of Research on Adolescence*, *11*(2), 199–224. DOI: 10.1111/1532-7795.00010.

Pople, L. (2010). Responding to antisocial behaviour. In: D.J. Smith (ed.), *New Response to Youth Crime* (pp. 143–179). Portland, OR: Willan Publishing.

Pratt, T.C., Turner, M.G., & Piquero, A.R. (2004). Parental socialization and community context: A longitudinal analysis of the structural sources of low self-control. *Journal of Research in Crime and Delinquency*, *41*(3), 219–243. DOI: 10.1177/0022427803260270.

Przybylski, R. (2008). What works: Effective recidivism reduction and risk-focused prevention programs. Denver, CO: Colorado Division of Criminal Justice. http://dcj .state.co.us/ors/pdf/docs/ww08_022808.pdf.

Qasem, F.S., Mustafa, A.A., Kazem, N.A., & Shah, N.M. (1998). Attitudes of Kuwaiti parents toward physical punishment of children. *Child Abuse and Neglect*, *22*(12), 1189–1202.

Raudenbush, S.W. & Bryk, A.S. (1986). A hierarchical model for studying school effects. *Social Education*, *59*(1), 1–17.

Raudenbush, S.W. & Bryk, A.S. (2002). *Hierarchical Linear Models: Applications and Data Analysis Methods*, 2nd ed. Newbury Park, CA: Sage Publications, Inc.

Rebellon, C.J. (2002). Reconsidering the broken homes/delinquency relationship and exploring its mediation mechanism(s). *Criminology*, *40*(1), 103–136.

Rebellon, C.J., Straus, M.A., & Medeiros, R. (2008). Self-control in global perspective: An empirical assessment of Gottfredson and Hirschi's general theory within and across 32 national settings. *European Journal of Criminology*, *5*(3), 331–362. DOI: 10.1177/1477370808090836.

Rebellon, C.J. & Van Gundy, K. (2005). Can control theory explain the link between parental physical abuse and delinquency? A longitudinal analysis. *Journal of Research in Crime and Delinquency, 42*(3), 247–274. DOI: 10.1177/0022427804271926.

Reckless, W.C. (1967). *The Crime Problem*, 4th ed. New York: Appleton-Century-Croft.

Reed, E. (2008). Intimate partner violence: A gender-based issue? *American Journal of Public Health, 98*(2), 197–198. DOI: 10.2105/AJPH.2007.125765.

Reiss, A.J. (1951). Delinquency as the failure of personal and social controls. *American Sociological Review, 16*(2), 196–207.

Reynolds, W.M. (1982). Development of reliable and valid short forms of the Marlowe-Crowne Social Desirability Scale. *Journal of Clinical Psychology, 38*(1), 119–125.

Reza, A., Mercy, J.A., & Krug, E.G. (2001). Epidemiology of violent deaths in world. *Injury Prevention,* 7(2), 104–111. http://www.cdc.gov/ncipc/pub-res/Global%20Violence.pdf.

Roberts, J.V. (2000). Changing public attitudes towards corporal punishment: The effects of statutory reform in Sweden. *Child Abuse and Neglect, 24*(8), 1027–1035. DOI: 10.1016/S0145-2134(00)00155-1.

Robertson, A.A., Baird-Thomas, C., & Stein, J.A. (2008). Child victimization and parental monitoring as mediators of youth problem behaviors. *Criminal Justice and Behavior, 35*(6), 755–772. DOI: 10.1177/0093854808316096.

Rosario, M., Salzinger, S., Feldman, R.S., & Ng-Mak, D.S. (2003). Community violence exposure and delinquent behaviors among youth: The moderating role of coping. *Journal of Community Psychology, 31*(5), 489–512.

Runyan, D.K., Shankar, V., & Hassan, F. (2010). International variations in harsh child discipline. *Pediatrics, 126,* E701–E711. DOI: 10.1542/peds.2008-2374.

Rutter, M. (1981). The city and the child. *American Journal of Orthopsychiatry* , 51, 610–625.

Rutter, M., Quinton, D., & Hill, J. (1990). Adult outcomes of institution-reared children. Males and females compared. In: L.N. Robins & M. Rutter (Eds.), *Straight and Devious Pathways from Childhood to Adulthood* (pp. 135–157). Cambridge, UK: Cambridge University Press.

Ryan, R.M. & Deci, E.L. (2000). Intrinsic and extrinsic motivations: Classic definitions and new directions. *Contemporary Educational Psychology, 25*(1), 54–67. DOI: 10.1006/ceps.1999.1020.

Sampson, R.J. & Laub, J.H. (1993). *Crime in the Making: Pathways and Turning Points through Life*. Cambridge, MA: Harvard University Press.

Sarat, A. (2001). *When the State Kills: Capital Punishment and the American Condition*. Princeton, NJ: Princeton University Press.

Satcher, D. (1995). Violence as a public health issue. *Bulletin of the New York Academy of Medicine, 72*(1), 46–56.

Sawyer, R.K. (2001). Emergence in sociology: Contemporary philosophy of mind and some implications for social logical theory. *American Journal of Sociology, 107*(3), 551–585.

Schmalleger, F. & Bartollas, C. (2008). *Juvenile Delinquency*. Boston, MA: Pearson Education, Inc.

Schoepfer, A. & Piquero, A.R. (2006). Self-control, moral beliefs, and criminal activity. *Deviant Behavior, 27*(1), 51–71. DOI: 10.1080/01639690968326.

Schreiner, L. & Louis, M. (2006, November). Measuring engaged learning in college students: Beyond the borders of NSSE. https://www.semanticscholar.org/paper/Measuring-Engaged-Learning-in-College-Students%3A-the-Schreiner/27bfc924ebe4a9a0b40b2f66fe6282fdaaa14d8d. Paper presented at the annual meeting of the Association for the Study of Higher Education, Anaheim, CA.

Schroeder, R.D., Giordano, P.C., & Cernkovich, S.A. (2010). Adult child-parent bonds and life course criminality. *Journal of Criminal Justice, 38*(4), 562–571. DOI: 10.1016/j.jcrimjus.2010.04.027.

Schweinhart, L.J. (2007). Crime prevention by the high/scope pre-preschool program. *Victims and Offenders, 2*(2), 141–160.

Sellers, J., Kübler, D., Walter-Rogg, M., & Walks, A. (2012). *The Political Ecology of the Metropolis.* Essex, UK: ECPR Press.

Shadish, W.R., Cook, T.D., & Campbell, D.T. (2002). *Experimental and Quasi-Experimental Designs for Generalized Causal Inference.* Boston, MA: Houghton Mifflin Company.

Shaw, C. (1930[1966]). *The Jackroller: A Delinquent Boy's Own Story.* Chicago, IL: The University of Chicago Press.

Shaw, V.N. (2010). Crime and social control in Asia and the Pacific: An examination of larger social institutions and processes. *Criminal Justice Studies, 23*(4), 303–323. DOI: 10.1080/1478601X.2010.516526.

Shortt, J.W., Low, S., Capaldi, D.M., Eddy, J.M., & Tiberio, S.S. (2017). Predicting intimate partner violence for at-risk young adults and their romantic partners. Washington, DC: US Department of Justice. https://nij.ojp.gov/library/publications/predicting-intimate-partner-violence-risk-young-adults-and-their-romantic.

Singer, J.D. & Willett, J.B. (2003). *Applied Longitudinal Data Analysis: Modeling Change and Event Occurrence.* New York: Oxford University Press.

Singleton, R.A. & Straits, B.C. (1988). *Approaches to Social Research.* New York: Oxford University Press.

Smagur, K.E., Bogat, G.A., & Leveondosky, A.A. (2017). Gender role and gender as predictors of behavior problems in children exposed to intimate partner violence. *Journal of Family Violence, 32*(2), 157–168. DOI: 10.1007/s10896-016-9890-3.

Smith, C. & Thornberry, T.P. (1995). The relationship between childhood maltreatment and adolescent involvement in delinquency. *Criminology, 33*(4), 451–481. DOI: 10.1111/j.1745-9125.1995.tb01186.x.

Socolar, R.R.S. & Stein, R.E.K. (1995). Spanking of infants and toddlers: Maternal belief and practice. *Pediatrics, 95*(1), 105–111.

Sokol-Katz, J., Dunham, R., & Zimmerman, R. (1997). Family structure versus parental attachment in controlling adolescent deviant behavior: A social control model. *Adolescence, 32*(125), 199–215.

Sousa, C., Herrenkohl, T.I., Moylan, C.A., Tajima, E.A., Klika, J.B., Herrenkohl, R.C., & Russo, M.J. (2011). Longitudinal study on the effects of child abuse and children's exposure to domestic violence, parent-child attachments, and antisocial behavior in adolescence. *Journal of Interpersonal Violence, 26*(1), 111–136. DOI: 10.1177/0886260510362883.

Spano, R., Rivera, C., & Bolland, J.M. (2010). Are chronic exposure to violence and chronic violent behavior closely related: Developmental processes during adolescence. *Criminal Justice and Behavior, 37*(10), 1160–1179. DOI: 10.1177/0093854810377164.

Steffensmeier, D. & Streifel, C. (1991). Age, gender, and crime across 3 historical periods −1935, 1960, and 1985. *Social Forces, 69*(3), 869–894.

Steiker, C.S. & Steiker, J.M. (2017). Capital punishment. In: Erik Luna (Ed.), *Reforming Criminal Justice, vol. 4: Punishment, Incarceration, and Release* (pp. 147–168) Phoenix, AZ: The Academy for Justice.

Straus, M.A. (1991). Discipline and deviance: Physical punishment of children and violence and other crime in adulthood. *Social Problems, 38*(2), 133–154. DOI: 10.2307/800524.

Straus, M.A. (2001). *Beating the Devil out of Them: Corporal Punishment in American Families and Its Effects on Children*. New Brunswick, NJ: Transaction Publishers.

Straus, M.A. (2004a). Cross-cultural reliability and validity of the revised conflict tactics scales: A study of university student dating couples in 17 nations. *Cross-Cultural Research, 38*(4), 407–432.

Straus, M.A. (2004b). *True Primordial Violence: Corporal Punishment by Parents, Cognitive Development and Crime*. Walnut Creek, CA: Alta Mira Press.

Straus, M.A. (2009). The national context effect: An empirical test of the validity of cross-national research using unrepresentative samples. *Cross-Cultural Research, 43*(3), 183–205. DOI: 10.1177/1069397109335770.

Straus, M.A. (2010). Prevalence, societal causes, and trends in corporal punishment by parents in world perspective. *Law and Contemporary Problems, 73*(2), 1–30. DOI: 10.2307/25766385.

Straus, M.A. & Donnelly, D.A. (1994). *Beating the Devil Out of Them: Corporal Punishment in American Families*. New York: Lexington Books.

Straus, M.A., Douglas, E.M., & Medeiros, R.A. (2014). *The Primordial Violence: Spanking Children, Psychological Development, Violence, and Crime*. New York: Routledge.

Straus, M.A., Gelles, R.J., & Steinmetz, S.K. (1980). *Behind Closed Doors: Violence in the American Family*. New Brunswick, NJ: TransAction.

Straus, M.A., Hamby, S.L., Boney-McCoy, S., & Sugarman, D. (2010). Manual for the personal and relationships profile (PRP). Family Research Laboratory, Durham, NH: University of New Hampshire. http://pubpages.unh.edu/~mas2/.

Straus, M.A. & Members of the International Dating Violence Research Consortium. (2004). Prevalence of violence against dating partners by male and female university students worldwide. *Violence Against Women, 10*(7), 790–811. DOI: 10.1177/1077801204265552.

Straus, M.A. & Ramirez, I.L. (2000). Detailed research design for the International Dating Violence Study. Family Research Laboratory, Durham, NH: University of New Hampshire. http://pubpages.unh.edu/~mas2/detailed-research-design.htm.

Sutherland, E.H. (1974). *Criminology*. Philadelphia, PA: J.B. Lippincott Company.

Sutherland, E.H. & Cressey, D.R. (1978). *Criminology*. Philadelphia, PA: J.B. Lippincott Co.

Sweeten, G., Piquero, A.R., & Steinberg, L. (2013). Age and the explanation of crime, revisited. *Journal of Youth and Adolescence, 42*(6), 921–938. DOI: 10.1007/s10964-013-9926-4.

Swidler, A. (1986). Culture in action: Symbols and strategies. *American Sociological Review, 51*(2), 273–286. DOI:10.2307/2095521

Tang, C.S. (2006). Corporal punishment and physical maltreatment against children: A community study on Chinese parents in Hong Kong. *Child Abuse and Neglect, 30*(8), 893–907.

Taylor, C.A., Hamvas, L., & Paris, R. (2011). Perceived instrumentality and normativeness of corporal punishment use among black mothers. *Family Relations, 60*(1), 60–72. DOI: 10.1111/j.1741-3729.2010.00633.x.

Teague, R., Mazerolle, P., Legosz, M., & Sanderson, J. (2008). Linking childhood exposure to physical abuse and adult offending: Examining mediating factors and gendered relationships. *Justice Quarterly, 25*(2), 313–348. DOI: 10.1080/07418820802024689.

Thompson, W.E. & Dodder, R.A. (1983). Juvenile delinquency explained? A test of containment theory. *Youth and Society, 15*(2), 171–194.

Thompson, W.E. & Dodder, R.A. (1986). Containment theory and juvenile delinquency: A reevaluation through factor analysis. *Adolescence, 21*(82), 365–376.

Thornton, W.E., Voigt, L., & Harper, D.W. (2013). *Why Violence?* Durham, NC: Carolina Academic Press.

Tittle, C.R. & Meier, R.F. (1990). Specifying the SES/delinquency relationship. *Criminology, 28*(2), 271–299.

Turner, M.G., Hartman, J.L., & Bishop, D.M. (2007). Disadvantage in predicting life-course-persistent offending the effects of prenatal problems, family functioning, and neighborhood. *Criminal Justice and Behavior, 34*(10), 1241–1261. DOI: 10.1177/0093854807304829.

Unicef. (2016). Age matters! https://agemattersnow.org/downloads/YPL_Age_Matters_Final_Report_Oct2016.pdf.

United Nations. (2006a). *United Nations Study on Violence against Children A/61/299.* New York: United Nations.

United Nations. (2006b). World report on violence against children. http://www.unicef.org/violencestudy/reports.html.

United Nations. (2012). United Nations Office on Drugs and Crime homicide statistics. http://www.unodc.org/unodc/en/data-and-analysis/homicide.html.

United Nations Office on Drugs and Crime. (2020). Global study on homicide 2019: Homicide trends, patterns and criminal justice. https://www.unodc.org/unodc/en/data-and-analysis/global-study-on-homicide.html.

Urquiza, A.J. & Goodlin-Jones, B.L. (1994). Child sexual abuse and adult revictimization with women of color. *Violence and Victims, 9*(3), 223–232.

Vazsonyi, A.T. & Flannery, D.J. (1997). Early adolescent delinquent behaviors: Associations with family and school domains. *Journal of Early Adolescence, 17*(3), 271–293.

Vold, G.B., Bernard, T.J., & Snipes, J.B. (1998). *Theoretical Criminology*, 4th ed. New York: Oxford University Press.

Wang, J. (1998). Opportunity to learn: The impacts and policy implications. *Educational Evaluation and Policy Analysis, 20*(3), 137–156.

Welsh, B.C. & Farrington, D.P. (2007a). Scientific support for early prevention of delinquency and later offending. *Victims and Offenders, 2*(2), 125–140. DOI: 10.1080/15564880701263114.

Welsh, B.C. & Farrington, D.P. (2007b). Saving children from a life of crime: Toward a national strategy for early prevention. *Victims and Offenders, 2*(1), 1–20. DOI: 10.1080/15564880601087233.

Wen, L.S. & Goodwin, K.E. (2016). Violence is a public health issue. *Journal of Public Health Management and Practice, 22*(6), 503–505. DOI: 10.1097/PHH.0000000000000501.

Whipple, E.E. & Richey, C.A. (1997). Crossing the line from physical discipline to child abuse: How much is too much? *Child Abuse and Neglect, 21*(5), 431–444.

Whitbeck, L.B. (1999). Primary socialization theory: It all begins with the family. *Substance Use and Misuse, 34*(7), 1025–1032. DOI: 10.3109/10826089909039394.

White, J.R. (2017). *Terrorism & Homeland Security*, 9th ed. Belmont, CA: Wadsworth.

Widom, C.S. (1989). Child abuse, neglect, and adult behavior: Research design and findings on criminality, violence, and child abuse. *American Journal of Orthopsychiatry, 59*(3), 355–367. DOI: 10.1111/j.1939-0025.1989.tb01671.x

Widom, C.S. & Maxfield, M.G. (2001). *An Updated on the "Cycle of Violence."* Washington, DC: National Institute of Justice.

Wiecko, F.M. (2010). Research note: Assessing the validity of college samples: are students really that different? *Journal of Criminal Justice, 38*, 1186-1190. DOI: 10.1016/j.jcrimjus.2010.09.007

Wolfgang, M.E. & Ferracuti, F. (1967). *The Subculture of Violence: Towards an Integrated Theory in Criminology*. New York: Tavistock Publications.

Woodruff, K. & Lee, B. (2011). Identifying and predicting problem behavior trajectories among pre-school children investigated for child abuse and neglect. *Child Abuse and Neglect*, *35*(7), 491–503.

World Health Organization. (2002). World report on violence and health. Geneva, Switzerland: Krug, E., L.L. Dahlberg, J.A. Mercy, A.B. Zwi & R. Lozano.

Wright, J. & Cullen, F. (2001). Parental efficacy and delinquent behavior: Do control and support matter? *Criminology*, *39*(3), 677–705. DOI: 10.1111/j.1745-9125.2001.tb00937.x.

Wyatt, G.E. (1994). Sociocultural and epidemiological issues in the assessment of domestic violence. *Journal of Social Distress and Homelessness*, *3*(1), 7–21. DOI: 10.1007/BF02087356.

Xu, X., Zuo, X., Wang, X., & Han, S. (2009). Do you feel my pain? Racial group membership modulates empathic neural responses. *The Journal of Neuroscience*, *29*(26), 8525–8529. DOI: 10.1523/JNEUROSCI.2418-09.2009.

Zhang, M., Barreto, M., & Doyle, D. (2020). Stigma-based rejection experiences affect trust in others. *Social Psychological and Personality Science*, *11*(3) 1–9. DOI: 10.1177/1948550619829057. https://www.researchgate.net/publication/332054895_Stigma-Based_Rejection_Experiences_Affect_Trust_in_Others.

Zhang, M., Zhang, Y., & Kong, Y. (2019). Interaction between social pain and physical pain. *Brain Science Advances*, *5*(4), 265–273. DOI: 10.26599/BSA.2019.9050023.

Zolotor, A.J. & Puzia, M.E. (2010). Bans against corporal punishment: A systematic review of the laws, changes in attitudes and behaviours. *Child Abuse Review*, *19*(4), 229–247. DOI: 10.1002/car.1131.

Zolotor, A.J., Theodore, A.D., Chang, J.J., Berkoff, M.C., & Runyan, D. (2008). Speak softly-and forget the stick - Corporal punishment and child physical abuse. *American Journal of Preventive Medicine*, *35*(4), 364–369. DOI: 10.1016/j.amepre.2008.06.031.

Zolotor, A.J., Theodore, A.D., Runyan, D.K., Chang, J.J., & Laskey, A.L. (2011). Corporal punishment and physical abuse: Population-based trends for three-to-11-year-old children in the United States. *Child Abuse Review*, *20*(1), 57–66. DOI: 10.1002/car.1128.

Appendix

Table A.1 General Linear Hypothesis Tests for Comparing Models

models 2a and 0
H_0: $\gamma_{10} = \tau_{11} = \tau_{01} = 0$
Model 0: −2 Log Likelihood = 66148.608
Model 2a: −2 Log Likelihood = 63046.525
Change in −2 Log Likelihood = 3102.083
Change in df = 3
X^2 (df=3; α = .05) = 7.82

REJECT NULL

models 2b and 2a
H_0: $\gamma_{10} = \gamma_{20} = \tau_{11} = \tau_{01} = 0$
Model 2a: −2 Log Likelihood = 63046.525
Model 2b: −2 Log Likelihood = 63002.713
Change in −2 Log Likelihood = 43.812
Change in df = 1
X^2 (df=1; α = .05) = 3.84

REJECT NULL

Index

For Product Safety Concerns and Information please contact our EU
representative GPSR@taylorandfrancis.com
Taylor & Francis Verlag GmbH, Kaufingerstraße 24, 80331 München, Germany

www.ingramcontent.com/pod-product-compliance
Lightning Source LLC
LaVergne TN
LVHW021130300926
849160LV00010B/955

* 9 7 8 0 3 6 7 7 1 2 3 1 0 *